ACCELERATE THRU CONFLICT

The Missing Conversations...
Before It's Too Late

DR. CRAIG OVERMYER
WITH MIKE MONTGOMERY

Praise for *Accelerating Thru Conflict*

"*Accelerate Thru Conflict* captures the insights gained from a seasoned coach working in the trenches with Scale Ups. Craig offers practical guidelines for executive teams and leaders at every level to put into practice the skill of productive conflict, especially when friendship and organizational politics make it easier to avoid these conversations."

Verne Harnish, Founder, Entrepreneurs' Organization (EO) and author of *Scaling Up (Rockefeller Habits 2.0)*

"The skill of productive conflict is one of the most underrated qualities of a leader and the mark of a mature, highly engaged organizational culture. A culture where productive conflict is embraced is exceptionally prepared to navigate change and turbulence, and this book is a leadership treasure as it brilliantly inspires and educates readers on how to grow and thrive through productive, in-the-moment conflict skills."

Santiago Jaramillo, Emplify CEO/cofounder, and Best-Selling Coauthor of *Agile Engagement*

"After reading dozens of books on influence, leadership, negotiating and sales to learn how to grow Allure Medical from 10M to 60M, I can honestly say I wish I had *Accelerate Thru Conflict* years ago. This book is the missing link and addresses a massively overlooked opportunity in a rapid growth company. Thank you for this book. I am buying it for my team and mid-leaders. Dr. Overmyer, your practical wisdom never ceases to amaze."

Theresa LaBranche, MS, PA-C, MBA,
Chief Operational Officer, Allure Medical

"Dr. Overmyer has worked with Allure Medical on the concept of how to have healthy conversations around conflict management since 2017. During the time Dr. Overmyer has been involved with us, the company has increased 10x in size. He has led companywide keynotes on servant leadership, meditation and conflict management. He has also been instrumental in implementing positive changes through coaching key leaders within our company. I would recommend this book to any company that is growing and striving to have an amazing culture and unstoppable leadership structure!"

Traci Grossman, MS, PA-C, Allure Medical

"In an increasingly dark and polarized world where even the most powerful people in the world hurl insults at each other on social media and in the press, it's too easy to just ignore conflict. Craig Overmyer persuasively argues that an understanding of how to use conflict as a business tool is a key to business growth."

David Meerman Scott, business growth strategist, entrepreneur, and *Wall Street Journal* Best-Selling Author of eleven books including *Fanocracy*

"This is good and well written. We have worked with Dr. Craig 10+ years and he has been instrumental in helping our company scale up and work to achieve our BHAG!"

Jeff Kittle, President and CEO, Herman & Kittle Properties

"The role of all leadership in learning how to have 'in-the-moment conversations' and elevating conflict from passive aggressive to accountability and successful results is essential in any business that has in their business plan sustainable growth. Whether for-profit or not-for-profit, there is only so much one person, or even one team, can do. However, using a shared vision and creating the trust to have substantial conversations, hold each other accountable and work together for the entire organization excels the possibilities logarithmically.

"We need to, as leaders, slough off our social accountability ideas, avoid getting 'sucked into' daily operations and tolerating underperformance because it is more socially easier, but rather stick to the vision and continue to share this vision by perfecting our ability to acquiesce our non-conforming thoughts and restating our purpose because 'as the leadership goes, so the whole company goes.'"

Dr. Ray Ingham, CEO, Witham Hospital

"This book provides guidelines for you to practice In-The-Moment Conversations for productive conflict solutions before it's too late… with disengaged employees and underperforming teams."

Mike Ellis, VP of Regional Managers
Herman Kittle Properties

"Craig's approach to "scaling up" through productive conflict, as described in this book, has been instrumental in Birge & Held's growth from a small apartment owner with $100M in assets to one of the largest multi-family apartment owners in the Midwest with over 1 Billion AUM."

Tag Birge, CEO, Birge & Held

ACCELERATE THRU CONFLICT

The Missing Conversations…
Before It's Too Late

DR. CRAIG OVERMYER
WITH MIKE MONTGOMERY

Cultures That Work, Inc.
9640 Commerce Drive
Carmel, IN 46032

ISBN: 9780578613185

Printed in the United States of America

Dedication

To my wife Becky, my daughter Meghan and my granddaughter Hadley, whose loving presence teaches me to live mindfully in the moment. I hope this book will inspire a global community of mindful leaders who are dedicated to creating a future workforce that inspires meaningful work through compassionate people who are focused on a purpose greater than profit.

- Craig Overmyer

To those who trained me, tolerated my style and have my back.

- Mike Montgomery

Contents

You Need

To Build An

In-The-Moment
Conversations

Productive Conflict

Habit

To Accelerate
Business Growth.

As everyone knows, owners, executive leaders and managers are saddled with the burden of helping all employees with communication skills for conflict resolution that reduces the drama of differing behavioral styles and opinions.

Foreword

The golden rule has been handed down from generation to generation as we have been taught to *treat others as we want to be treated*. This is certainly a noble way that we should interact with others as it focuses on building harmony. Not only is this practiced inside the home, but it is alive and well inside in the workplace.

In my experience of working with hundreds of leaders and managers in organizations of all sizes, I have often seen how conflict is avoided at all costs by others within an organization to build harmony. In fact, having difficult conversations with their teams is one of the most avoided responsibilities leaders and managers have.

And yet, not having those difficult conversations in order to make simple course adjustments in behavior and performance can often lead to longer-term drama and disruption, not only on an individual level but it can also become a cancer of the culture of an organization.

There are many reasons managers avoid having difficult conversations. Some organizations haven't built the necessary trust within the organization that is key to having these important conversations. In other situations, the managers merely want to be liked by their teams and may believe this will help create positive morale and culture.

But the goal of building a high-performance team isn't just making sure everyone likes each other.

It should be building a team that has mutual respect for one another with each individual contributing to their best ability and in alignment with the overall mission and vision of the company.

A quick review of an income statement will show that personnel costs are one of the largest expenses in a business. Yet managing this significant investment is one of the least planned and ineffectively executed.

Rarely will you find a business that doesn't perform routine maintenance on their property and equipment to keep it at optimal performance. Yet this is not something that is applied to their people. The reason? Leaders and managers have not been properly trained on how to do this type of routine maintenance. They don't have the tools.

The old adage "iron sharpens iron" is exactly what Craig Overmyer and the contributing authors of *Accelerate Thru Conflict*—Mike Montgomery and the Cultures That Work team—teach leaders and managers.

Their *In-the-Moment Conversations and Productive Conflict* methodologies will sharpen leaders of an organization to help it scale and grow more quickly and effectively. The leaders will have the tools they need.

Friction within every organization is unavoidable; however, reducing it is critical for the organization to run at peak performance. *Accelerate Thru Conflict* couldn't be more aptly named.

The reader will learn to have *In-The-Moment Conversations* using Craig and his team's research-based tools and methodologies, which will accelerate resolution and, ultimately, revolution.

For as conflict and friction are reduced and the organization is aligned with its overall vision, the business can scale more efficiently and effectively.

This book is long overdue in the leadership and management curriculum as it provides practical advice and steps on how to begin developing the skill that is lacking in many managers and leaders.

It's time to move your organization from congenial to collegial by having great tools at your side so you can be aware of what's real, reflect on what's ideal, gain insight for solutions and take action for ideal results.

As the CEO of a high-growth HR business and author of the Amazon best-selling *Go Slow to Grow Fast*, I am proud to offer this foreword and strongly support the outstanding work provided herein.

- Brent Tilson

Introduction

"Only three things happen naturally in organizations: friction, confusion, and under-performance. Everything else requires leadership." - Peter Drucker

What if…leaders who were accountable for functions and processes that drive your business successfully had the courage to seek accountability and hold one another accountable? Imagine a workplace without drama and the need for an intervention by someone with ultimate authority, such as a boss, an owner, a CEO or President, *even* if they are prepared to do so.

In this book, you will discover how to raise the quality of conversations to **accelerate thru conflict** by learning how to create the habit of putting into practice *In-The-Moment Conversations*™ productive conflict solutions *before* it's too late; that is, before the stakes are high, disengagement rises and performance slacks off, requiring a critical conversation with the manager or boss.

Why? The momentum of compounding success as you scale up depends on it!

Everyone must face the natural "friction, confusion, and underperformance" of growth when scaling up.

Moment by moment, the quality of conversations and how everyone in your culture deals with conflict accelerates or decelerates the momentum of "the flywheel effect"[1] for exponential growth.

At Cultures That Work, we help busy leaders at every level of your organization learn practical tools for having brief, impactful conversations with colleagues and peers to encourage each other to seek accountability to do what matters most to achieve exponential growth.

Your leaders and managers are probably **not participating** in effective conversations for productive conflict solutions. Also, you're probably **not training** employees with the skill of practicing productive conflict solutions with their colleagues through the self-leadership it takes to transform "friction, confusion, and underperformance."

Why This Book Is for Scale-Ups

When scaling up, the increased complexity of adding new people, upgrading systems and evolving processes increases the natural experience of "friction, confusion, and underperformance."

It is crucial to overcome the cultural entropy that results from scaling up. The head of the company and executive leadership team need to model how to courageously give and receive feedback through In-The-Moment Conversations productive conflict.

Leadership is not just a functional role. It is defined as anyone who "takes responsibility for finding the potential in people and processes, and who has the courage to develop that potential."[2]

Mindful leadership is the capacity to be fully present and engaged in the moment, with equanimity. High-quality conversations are based on assuming mutual trust, respect and accountability.

This is a *guidebook* for increasing the momentum of compounding success through mindful leadership at every level. You can learn to accelerate thru conflict and make it safe for colleagues to encourage colleagues to achieve the higher purpose of your growth firm.

Why Practice Productive Conflict

The owner and executive team need to be focused on "fusing" their culture with their brand to create a unique presence in the marketplace[3] which can only be achieved when they are free from being dragged into daily operations. The owner and executive team must focus primarily on making new deals, on rapidly changing market dynamics and on the customer experience of value. Then, they can fulfill the higher purpose and expectations of the business.

The vice presidents, directors and managers need to focus on coaching teams to seek accountability with one another as colleagues so the managers can continue to refine systems, processes and procedures.

The executive leadership team must strive to also be a cohesive team, modeling for everyone in the culture how to be trustworthy, master conflict, make commitments, hold one another accountable and focus on collective results.[4]

After the essential skill of creating vulnerability-based trust between colleagues in the senior executive team is in place, the most challenging competencies for the culture to put into practice are the communication skills to master conflict so that the owner and senior team are free to do market-facing activities.

Why Is This a Challenge?

The senior executive team's ability to debate and have productive conflict is an essential competency for cohesive teams.

The executive team must model the ability to practice candid productive conflict. Then, everyone else in the culture will know what it means to seek accountability for the collective results of the company.

However, most of us are conditioned, through social norms, to be friendly with colleagues and peers at work and avoid conflict. This avoidance will lead to destructive conflict behaviors.

It is much more comfortable to be congenial and friendly at work than to engage in much-needed productive conflict. It is much more of a challenge to be collegial, without concern for roles. Productive conflict solutions need to be more about being collegial and less about being congenial.

Why This New Habit for Your Culture

David Rock, who coined the term *NeuroLeadership,* defines company culture as "shared everyday habits."[5]

For firms that are scaling up, we align with the concept of *Mastering the Rockefeller Habits* by Verne Harnish.[6] Rockefeller Execution Habits are focused on the most important priorities and using data to confirm the achievement of those priorities. The habit of maintaining meeting rhythms will synchronize teams to be mindful to measure and achieve the shared vision.

When scaling up, it is especially important to practice high-quality conversations. The opportunities for these conversations arise when there are possible indications of misalignment. This could occur ad hoc, or after daily huddles, and during weekly, quarterly and annual planning meetings.

Every day, moment by moment, between colleagues, there are innumerable interactions that impact the achievement of the higher purpose of your company to meet or exceed the expectations of your customers.

During these moments, giving and receiving feedback could create a threatening, stressful mental state, causing colleagues to often waver between unproductive, productive and destructive conflict.

In an article on this subject, "Using Neuroscience to Make Feedback Work and Feel Better," David Rock and his coauthors summarized the research on the science behind giving and receiving feedback and found that "by switching from giving feedback to asking for it, organizations can tilt their culture toward continuous improvement."[7]

After thousands of hours of coaching and training, it is our experience as coaches that colleagues want and need feedback as they face the complexity of scaling up.

Just like organisms in nature that need feedback to survive, scaling up organizations need feedback to stay alive and well when facing the inevitable changes in systems and processes when battling the natural friction, confusion and underperformance during growth.

However, the research cited in this article indicates that the stress for colleagues who need to give feedback is actually more stressful, neurologically, than for those receiving feedback.

Our Four STEP In-The-Moment Conversations provides a systematic method that will equip colleagues to ask for and seek accountability to keep getting better together.

In-The-Moment Conversations™ is a brain-friendly feedback tool that alleviates the threat caused by giving and receiving feedback. These high-quality conversations are essential for scaling up your organization; accelerate thru conflict to accelerate the momentum of business growth.

These are the missing conversations.

In-The-Moment Conversations
is defined as a collaborative
methodology to guide colleagues
through a systematic process for
timely productive conflict solutions.

How does it work?

Clear your mind from the background noise to
expand **awareness** of the real challenge before you.

Reflect on possibilities for ideal conflict solutions
and discover an energizing shared vision of
possibilities.

Inspire and capture new **insights** from successes
and/or failures, and then commit to be in alignment
toward the shared vision.

Seek mutual trust, respect and accountability
to **execute** new habits for accelerating growth
momentum.

Four STEP In-The-Moment Conversations Guidelines

1. Seize the Moment and Regain Focus

- Clear your mind from the background noise
- Expand **awareness** of the real challenge

2. Remember the Future and Craft a Shared Vision

- **Reflect** on possibilities for ideal conflict solutions
- Discover an energizing shared vision of possibilities

3. Learn from the Past to Build Organizational Alignment

- Inspire new **insights** from lessons learned
- Commit to alignment toward the shared vision

4. Seek Accountability to Champion Execution Habits

- Seek mutual trust, respect and accountability
- **Execute** new habits for accelerating growth momentum

Seize the Moment and Regain Focus: become aware of the real challenge

Suppose someone experiences a challenging conflict that creates the need for a conversation between colleagues. Take a time-out, to observe the realities, even the brutal facts, by using data or feedback. Stay even keeled. Think of the real conflict or challenge as news, not necessarily bad news or good news. Just news.

Using a sports metaphor, often there is a need for the team to take a time-out to make sure everyone is aware of the realities, such as the score, some misalignment with the intended play or the amount of time left on the clock. Such a defining moment warrants a time-out, to clear your mind of distractions and regain your focus as a team seeking to accomplish a common goal.

A metaphor of a real challenge is the physical feeling you get when the wheels of your car are out of alignment, causing some vibration and difficulty in the steering. The alignment activity is regular maintenance to transform friction, confusion and underperformance.

For airline pilots, it's the need for a captain and copilot to have a conversation about a dilemma or conflict—perhaps a warning light or some other indicator—that needs to be resolved before it becomes a crisis.

These are the moments to have the missing In-The-

Moment Conversations to address misalignments before it's too late.

Remember the Future and Craft a Shared Vision: reflect on the ideal vision

Rather than being gripped by the friction, confusion and underperformance that create conflicts, focus on possible solutions. How do you focus on solutions? By remembering the future!

Most sports coaches give a pep talk, helping the team remember the goal and what it will be like and feel like when the goal is achieved.

When we are just focused on the problem, the stress response sets up a fight or flight state. The brain chemistry is overwhelmed by the sympathetic nervous system response of cognitive, perceptual and emotional impairment. When faced with complexity from growth, individuals or teams can be stressed.[8]

Describing the vision in detail activates a brain chemistry in the parasympathetic nervous system, a response that is characterized by renewal, energy, positive mood, increased engagement and higher levels of performance.[9]

It is vital to get into that optimal performance zone and to avoid becoming overwhelmed by the "friction, confusion and underperformance" experienced by scale-ups.

Remembering the future (a vivid vision) is about staying energized toward meaningful work and overcoming the inevitable barriers to growth caused by the complexity of scaling up.

Learn from the Past to Build Organizational Alignment: gain insights from lessons learned

During this stage of the conversation, new insights will emerge. Literally, new neural pathways will be developed over time.[10]

Like the sports coach drawing up a new play on the clipboard, the individual or team gets back into alignment.

This occurs because each person in this dialogue is self-evaluating and asking themselves, "What lessons did we learn? What could I do, or what could the team do, to improve? What have we learned from both successes and failures?"

The best coaches stimulate insight in others and don't just tell people what to do. They inspire a growth mind-set. They know the difference between "Hear-to-Fix; Tell-to-Solve" and "Listen-to-Learn; Ask-to-Empower."

In this "Listen-to-Learn; Ask-to-Empower" dialogue, you will listen to learn the perspectives of others. Each person should create a climate where it is safe to speak up, welcoming differing opinions. This is the time to ask questions to empower each other to gain insights about the new possibilities for solutions to do what matters most.

Everyone agrees to be in alignment to do what matters most and are ready to make a promise to seek accountability.

Seek Accountability to Champion Execution Habits: accelerate the momentum of growth by executing the "if-then" habit formation

When team members are engaged in productive conflict solutions by using this model for a collaborative dialogue, it generates an energy to act and champion higher performance.

Most great coaches are so good at this kind of dialogue that when the team breaks from the huddle, the energy can be amazing. The team keeps getting better together to overcome great obstacles.

Now, magnetized to achieve the shared vision, with everyone in alignment, intense motivation has been tapped into and will inspire team members to do the hard work and take actions to execute on the plan to achieve the shared vision.

Remember, this dialogue is not about just hearing what the conflict is and then fixing it. That approach can stimulate immediate short-term compliance at the expense of long-term engagement.

Listen to learn the perspectives of others, and then ask open-ended questions to empower them to think. This will inspire discretionary effort, to do that little bit of extra beyond what is expected.

This is the time to build new habits using the "if-then" habit formation technique that can accelerate the momentum of business growth.

Not Casual, Not Crisis

In-The-Moment Conversations are not yet in the zone of crisis conversations, nor are they casual. They are important conversations most of us have never been trained to practice!

Your culture needs to equip everyone to address conflicts—concerns that matter the most—moment by moment, throughout the workday, before it's too late, employees disengage, and business momentum decelerates!

Here are examples of concerns, those "defining moments" of conflict:

- Customer experience is substandard

- Lack of follow-up on promised deliverables

- Personality conflicts create intense drama

- Miscommunication between departments

- Avoidance of accountability or responsibility

- Disengaged employees

- The need to conduct hard conversations
  when someone is not holding to the standards

Too much friction, confusion, and underperformance negatively impact employee engagement.

In-The-Moment Conversations productive conflict solutions begins when the executive team becomes healthy and aligned.[11]

Often, friendships, organizational politics or familial relationships lead to false harmony and unproductive or destructive conflict.[12]

Unproductive conflict is false harmony where the conflict is hidden. It's comfortable to avoid issues, but it is artificial.

Destructive conflict occurs when conflict events trigger automatic assumptions, biases and beliefs that lead to destructive responses, disengagement and underperformance.

Productive conflict requires self-awareness, self-leadership, self-management and empathy for colleagues by honoring each other's styles. This makes it safe to speak up and face challenges by practicing In-The-Moment Conversations.

Part 1

Conflict Impacts Momentum

"The better able team members are to engage, speak, listen, hear, interpret and respond constructively, the more likely their teams are to leverage conflict rather than being leveraged by it."[13]

-This is a quote from Craig Runde and Tim Flanagan, authors of Becoming a Conflict Competent Leader, *a must read for anyone interested in the subject of conflict!*

Accelerating Momentum

Tag Birge and Andrew Held are real estate attorneys by trade and childhood friends. When they launched Birge & Held (B&H) in 2008, it was exciting. Their first strategic plan was on the proverbial napkin from the coffee shop!

When they closed their first deal on an apartment complex, they realized, "Wow, we need lots of people to help!"

As a startup, the pressure to lease and manage the property was like pushing this "giant, heavy, enormous flywheel."[14]

Have you been involved in a startup? If so, you know the enormous pressure and what it feels like to get the flywheel started, and to keep it going.

Back then, Andrew and Tag kept *pusssssshhhhhing* to execute the newly formed strategies and keep cash flowing from an increasing number of happy tenants in new locations. The momentum of B&H business growth ***accelerated*** quarter by quarter!

Tag and Andrew learned that the pushing of the B&H flywheel could only continue to accelerate momentum only if they trained others to *pusssssshhhhh.* They couldn't do it on their own.

Today, they are diligently training the key leaders in business acumen and leadership skills. Tag and Andrew engage the executive leadership team to practice In-The-Moment Conversations for Productive Conflict solutions.

As of 2019, B&H owns over $1,000,000,000 in assets, at 45 well-managed properties, located in 7 states, with over 275 employees and counting! The momentum will keep going only if Tag and Andrew create a feedback-rich culture of accountability by using the Mindful Leadership at Every Level Training.

The strategy is no longer on a napkin; it's on Aligntoday's virtual platform for the Scaling Up Scoreboard. The B&H executive leadership team practices quarterly strategic thinking/execution planning by following the system found in *Scaling Up* by Verne Harnish.[15]

As their Scaling Up Coach, I guide them to leverage the Scaling Up Growth Tools, including the Rockefeller Habits Checklist and the famous One Page Strategic Plan.

The Birge & Held Flywheel Components

Identify Exciting Multi-family Opportunities

- Create a High Standard of Living for Residents

- Identify Value Creating Opportunities for New Properties

- Secure Long-Term Financing through Investors

- Build Well-Capitalized Improvement Plans

- Continuously Reinvest in Properties

- Provide Best Practices of Responsive Property Management Teams

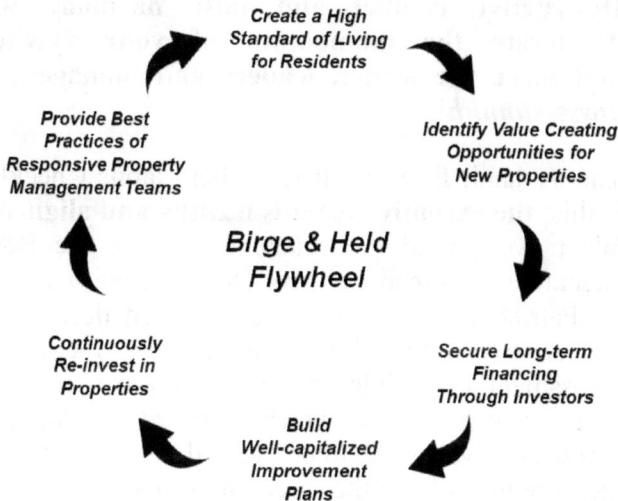

Create a High Standard of Living for Residents

Identify Value Creating Opportunities for New Properties

Provide Best Practices of Responsive Property Management Teams

Birge & Held Flywheel

Continuously Re-invest in Properties

Secure Long-term Financing Through Investors

Build Well-capitalized Improvement Plans

"Once you fully grasp how to create flywheel momentum in your particular circumstance, and apply that understanding with creativity and discipline, you get the power of strategic compounding."[16] - Jim Collins

Disciplined People

The flywheel is a way of thinking to determine how your growth firm creates momentum for strategic compounding. The B&H executive leaders developed a strategy that creates an almost unstoppable momentum as they strive toward achieving their 2028 Big Hairy Audacious Goal (BHAG)[17] of 450 Leaders serving middle-class families in 30,000 apartment homes.

What decelerates this momentum? The answer is the same for you as well!

Destructive conflict and false harmony will decelerate the momentum of your flywheel and force the owner, leaders and managers to *pussssshhhhh*!

The #1 habit from the Rockefeller Habits Checklist is this: **the executive team is healthy and aligned.**[18] When we started the coaching process, the B&H executive team read *The Five Dysfunctions of a Team* by Patrick Lencioni. Then, to go even deeper, the executive team took John Wiley & Sons, Inc. online assessment and training program *The Five Behaviors of a Cohesive Team*, which is based on Patrick's work. They were able to compare their team with the measurements from the research on 6,400 leaders of the most cohesive teams. This process revealed three areas for improvement:

  1. Trust One Another

  2. Engage in **Conflict** around Ideas

  3. Hold One Another **Accountable**

These dysfunctions are issues for many scale-ups facing the complexity of growth!

The B&H Executive Leadership Team members learned each other's styles and realized how important it was for the executive leaders to practice the disciplines of cohesive teams: "as the leadership team goes, so the whole company goes."[19]

Of course, it goes without saying that trust is the foundation for all relationships. The B&H team wanted to build trust and learn to improve how they engage in conflict around ideas.

Overcoming the fear of conflict is often the behavior that needs to improve for most of the senior leaders of scale ups. Many factors impact the scaling up momentum.

The research from Daniel Goleman, Richard Boyatzis and Annie McKee confirms that the Emotional Intelligence competency of Conflict Management is one of the most challenging leadership competencies to master.[20]

Unproductive avoidance of conflict or destructive conflict will negatively impact momentum, even if you have significant levels of trust!

Lack of development of productive conflict solutions makes it unlikely you will fully develop the much-needed skill of seeking accountability.

When unproductive or destructive conflict occurs, the founder of a startup, the CEO or President will *pussssshhhhh* the flywheel themselves through their own efforts and that of a handful of loyal people.

Fill in this statement:

"If this is going to get done right, I'll just do it ____!"

If you automatically thought *myself*, then I challenge you to assess and develop your Emotional Intelligence competency of Conflict Management.

Why? Because as you scale up, if you're a boss, the complexity makes it impossible for you to fix everything. Also, for colleagues, friendship bonds are formed when facing the inevitable scaling up battles, and that makes it even more challenging to have healthy conflict with those friends who have gone into battle with you!

"In essence, your executive team needs to have a level of trust that permits true debate and constructive conflict. What prevents this in large companies is politics; what prevents it in growth firms is friendships. Members of the team must embrace its diversity (the more the better) and be willing to challenge each other in making decisions and exposing the brutal facts."[21]

What about you and your executive team? Do you have healthy debate and constructive conflict?

Engaging Productive Conflict

Tag and Andrew made the decision to replicate the newly developed productive conflict solutions discipline practiced by the executive team with leaders at every level.

For example, they had training for those who were accountable for complex processes such as new acquisitions and asset management. In addition, B&H had processes that moved across functions such as construction teams, property management teams and facilities maintenance teams.

Regional Managers and the Property Management

teams are accountable and responsible for day-to-day actions that drive the economic engine described in the B&H flywheel. These leaders were trained to practice the discipline of productive conflict solutions.

Tag and Andrew wanted to create a disciplined culture "with less hierarchy" as described by Jim Collins.[22]

Therefore, they lead In-The-Moment Conversations productive conflict solutions with their executive team. These leaders become a model for the culture to address conflict before it becomes a crisis. Like that, the Regional Managers and Director of Training are accountable to ensure productive conflict solutions becomes an integral habit of the leadership DNA of the culture that impacts high-level functions and key processes that drive the flywheel momentum.[23]

Productive Conflict Profile

Our social conditioning makes it a "threat" state to be in conflict with friends and to face organizational politics. Often at work, we will opt for false harmony to avoid the pain of dealing with conflicting opinions, priorities and styles.

Or, we will launch into destructive conflict through our automatic negative thoughts (ANTs), judgments, biases and perceptions of others.[24] (More about this later!)

It is important for you and your teams to understand each other's styles during conflict and uncover the hidden strengths and challenges that each person must face when engaged in a conflict.

The Productive Conflict Profile by John Wiley & Sons, Inc. is refreshing and new. The profile generated uncovers how destructive conflict can be like a cancer throughout your culture.[25] Destructive conflict will fuel disengagement that decelerates your economic engine described by your flywheel.

An important focus of this book is to help you understand how executive teams and managers who are accountable for functions and processes across departments, divisions or teams may accelerate thru conflict. Then they model how to engage in productive conflict solutions to colleagues throughout the culture. This inspires the whole culture to keep building the momentum of business growth as it scales up, without the intervention of a boss.

Additional resources on pages 46 through 57 in the book *Scaling Up*, you will get help completing the Function Accountability Chart (FACe) and the Process Accountability Chart (PACe).[26] These tools are essential to answering the following questions: Who is accountable? Who is responsible? Who has authority?

Even if you have not developed your flywheel, your business is either accelerating or decelerating the momentum for scaling up, at every moment, through every interaction, by all your employees.

Whatever it takes to build the momentum to grow your business, you're likely to face the same problem, the missing conversations.

In-The-Moment Conversations™ Named

Alycen Williams, an exceptionally skilled Regional Manager at Birge & Held, shared this idea with me after a training event.

Alycen said, "I'm working with a manager who has not mastered conflict and just doesn't know how to have an **in-the-moment conversation.**"

When I heard Alycen use that term, I was inspired to use that name for the intellectual property developed by the CTW team and our partners. The Birge & Held managers were trained to make it easier for them to master In-The-Moment Conversations that result in proactive productive conflict solutions.

The rest of this book is designed for you to discover how to equip colleagues at every level to **Accelerate Thru Conflict.** You will learn how to implement the Four STEP model for In-The-Moment Conversations productive conflict solutions in your organization.

Are you leveraging conflict, or is conflict leveraging you? The answer to that question will impact the momentum of your business flywheel, the engagement of your teams and your personal well-being at work.

Part 2

Transform Friction into Productive Conflict

Tipping the Scales of Conflict

When the vice president in charge of construction for a real estate firm that owned over 150 apartment complexes answered the phone on a Saturday evening at about 9 p.m., he was surprised, and a bit annoyed.

The maintenance supervisor at one of their properties noticed a crack in a newly installed bathtub. He knew this would prevent the new tenant from moving in if it didn't get repaired.

When the VP asked him, "Charlie, why did you call me? You are a professional. What would you do to fix the problem?" Charlie responded, "I could go to Home Depot and get everything I need, and it will be repaired."

Exasperated, the VP said, "Great, Charlie, go ahead and do that. But I need to ask you something. Why didn't you call the property manager?"

Charlie said, very sarcastically, "Every time I ask to go to buy supplies for repairs, Sally complains that I don't have authority to buy anything, our budgets are tight, and we won't hit our numbers if we overspend. There is no need to try to talk with her. She just doesn't listen."

PRODUCTIVE CONFLICT
Requires self-leadership from colleagues to honor each other's sytle
and make sure it's safe during In-The-Moment Conversations.

UNPRODUCTIVE CONFLICT
This is false harmony. The conflict is hidden. It's comfortable to avoid issues, but artificial.

DESTRUCTIVE CONFLICT
Conflict events trigger automatic biased thoughts, which in turn trigger destructive responses.

HOW WILL YOU CHANGE YOUR RESPONSE TO CONFLICT?

In this situation, Sally was tipping the scales toward unproductive false harmony and didn't want to rock the boat. For Charlie, the scales tipped the other way because of his automatic thoughts ("There is no need to try to talk with her. She just doesn't listen."). These automatic thoughts led to his withdrawal from Sally which is a destructive conflict response. What examples come to mind in your organization?

What's it like for you when the scales tip back and forth, rather than being balanced? How would this tipping back and forth impact the business flywheel?

"Conflict is an absolutely critical piece for you to demonstrate you care for your team."[27]

Alden Mills, U.S. Navy Seal, Retired

Too Much Friction

The friction between the property manager and maintenance supervisor continued to tip the scales, back and forth between unproductive and destructive conflict, and negatively impacted the apartments being rent-ready.

When there is too much friction, the scales tip from unproductive false harmony to destructive conflict. It's like both the property manager and the maintenance supervisor put the brakes on the momentum of the business. There was lost time, lost revenue and distractions for the VP that decelerated the momentum of the flywheel.

The friction between the property manager and the maintenance supervisor impacts not only the new residents but also the financial results.

Whenever a VP is dragged into daily operations due to friction between two colleagues, as in this example, it will take their mind and time off higher-level strategies and bigger-picture thinking.

A fresh concept about the "friction" that naturally occurs in any work situation comes from Richard Barrett, founder of the Barrett Values Centre, an organization that specializes in assessing Cultural Entropy®:

> Cultural entropy measures the internal frictions, relationship issues, structural misalignments and system problems existing in your organization that are working against

the achievement of your mission, vision and strategy.[28]

I often share the following references during the first two-day strategic thinking/execution planning event for firms that are scaling up.

In *Corporate Culture and Performance,* John P. Kotter and James L. Heskett show that companies with strong adaptive cultures based on shared values outperformed other companies by a significant margin. Over an eleven-year period, the companies that emphasized all stakeholders grew four times faster than companies that did not. The authors also found that these companies had job creation rates seven times higher, stock prices that grew 12 times faster and profit performance that was 750 times higher than companies that did not have shared values and adaptive cultures.[29]

In *Built to Last,* Jim Collins and Jerry I. Porras show that companies that consistently focused on building strong corporate cultures over a period of several decades outperformed companies that did not by a factor of 6 and outperformed the general stock market by a factor of 15.[30]

The CEO of this scaling up firm commissioned me to assess their culture by leveraging the Cultural Values Assessment (CVA) report from the Barrett Values Centre.

What follows is a small, but impactful section of the analysis in the extensive 21-page executive summary of that report, with recommendations for this company.

The CEO wanted to know, "Why is there drama and a failure to deliver quality products on time, for the right price?" This is some of the narrative from their Cultural Values Assessment:

> **When your organization was rating the current culture, twelve percent of all votes were for potentially limiting values. This level of entropy reflects issues requiring cultural or structural adjustment. It is important to reduce the level of entropy to 5%–10% to improve performance.**
>
> - **Systems and processes are rigid, and employees lack the autonomy and resources to fully support their efforts.**
>
> - **There is a shortage of clear direction, and people are overworked.**
>
> - **Internal divisions hinder the flow of communication and cooperation across the organization.**[31]

After debriefing the report, the CEO remarked, "This helps me understand that managers and employees across functions are struggling with our systems and processes. We are bigger, but not big enough to handle all the new business."

"What could happen if you don't address this entropy?" I asked.

The CEO continued: "Well, the ball gets dropped on delivering what we promised to our customers. The managers from each department get an earful from their employees who are frustrated with the employees in the other departments, who aren't 'pulling their weight.' Then, I get sucked into this battle because the managers blame each other for the customer complaints. There are too few higher-quality conversations between the departments' managers and employees to hold one another accountable, to keep the standards and to deliver what we promised, at the quality level expected by our customers."

I paused for a moment and then asked, "How is this impacting the momentum for your business growth?"

"Are you kidding?!" said the CEO. "The cultural entropy, as you call it, definitely has impacted our business. It's like putting the brakes on the momentum of our business growth.

"For example, I got a call from a client that had one hour to fix a problem. If we didn't fix it, it would cost $75,000 a minute. The customer trusted us for years. They got a part that didn't meet their standards, so they felt betrayed.

"We went on-site and resolved the crisis. But the real problem, now that I think about it, was the cultural entropy that was going unchecked."

As I reflected on what he said, I shared this: "Yes, avoiding conflict with peers was at a higher value than keeping the promise to the customer. Avoiding conflict is a symptom that false harmony has become a habit between peers. Things need to be said to keep the standards which fulfill the promise to the customer."

The CEO had an insight. "That is right. The manager did not want to experience the stress of engaging in conflict with his peers or with the client. He hoped it would be OK. Again, that puts the brakes on our business!"

I responded, "The report we received, and the story you have shared, helps me to know that your culture would benefit by learning how to go beyond the social norms to avoid conflict. They can learn how to honor the social conditioning and practice productive conflict solutions. This includes a method for communicating with some discomfort, right in the moment with a colleague, to hold the promise to the customer."

The CEO continued to share his insights: "I can tell you this, growing so quickly used to be exciting and fun. Now, I wake up in the night, wondering what could go off track and create drama with our people that creates chaos for our clients."

I replied, "When we look at the report, your culture is asking for help. This report was generated by input from the employees to describe their experience of personal values they bring to work, the experience of what is valued in the current culture and their perception of the desired culture that would reduce stress in daily operations."

I continued, "The next section of the executive summary from the CVA will show you what your employees need and want to experience. A majority of the employees want to find a way to hold one another accountable."

The executive summary from the CVA said this:

The employees in your organization want to live the values of teamwork, continuous improvement, customer satisfaction, community involvement and accountability.[32]

Because of the measurable results from the CVA, and the coaching with the CEO and executive team, we launched a live training event. They leveraged a virtual platform to make the training stick. The course is titled:

Mindful Leadership at Every Level
In-The-Moment Conversations
Productive Conflict Solutions

Leaders and managers learned to put into practice what it takes to seek accountability and to empower one another to know who is accountable for key functions and processes that have been strained by growth.

As is often the case, fear of conflict emerges as a significant communication barrier for firms scaling up. After about six months of training and coaching, this firm equipped leaders at every level to transform the natural friction experienced between departments.

According to the *HBR* [Harvard Business Review] *Guide to Dealing with Conflict* by Amy Gallo, there are two types of people with respect to conflict: people who avoid conflict and people who seek conflict.[33]

The employees whose temperament is to avoid conflict must be afforded a psychologically safe environment to speak up, be vulnerable and stay focused on the higher purpose of the organization.

Employees whose temperament is to seek conflict must be trained to listen more actively and to make it safe to be vulnerable to admit and learn from mistakes. This makes it possible to transform too much friction from destructive conflict into productive conflict.

Productive conflict solutions can emerge when the owner, executive leadership team and key leaders reduce cultural entropy.

Make it safe to be open with one another and address the natural friction of scaling up through In-The-Moment Conversations.

A key takeaway here is that conflict does not have to be negative.

It's all a matter of leadership and how you choose to use it.

Friction is natural and necessary for growth, but what does it take to transform friction that shows up as either false harmony or destructive conflict into productive conflict?

A stellar example of someone who knows how to transform destructive conflict into productive conflict is Jeff Kittle, President of Herman & Kittle Properties (HKP).

Jeff has led the company to more than double the number of properties owned and triple the employee count since 2010. They are a national leader in affordable housing. Jeff has learned to instill—within leaders at every level in his culture—what he calls "dynamic friction."

Serving as the HKP Scaling Up coach for 10 years, I have observed how Jeff and his senior management team have developed the exceptional ability to practice productive conflict solutions through In-The-Moment Conversations. For example, when the monthly senior management meeting begins and people gather around the conference room table, in a friendly yet professional atmosphere, the team still knows the need to engage in dynamic friction to face the innumerable challenges of scaling up.

As the principal owner and President, Jeff demonstrates exceptional emotional intelligence when leading the meeting. Jeff primarily listens to learn and asks questions to empower others to think, debate and challenge one another.

Because there is a high level of trust, Jeff will ask questions to empower the team to share diverse ideas.

The best quality answers live within the process of debate, for example, productive conflict solutions.

He often inspires debate about crucial decisions that have to be made so the company can stay on track while achieving the priorities for the quarter, the initiatives for the year and the longer-term Big Hairy Audacious Goal. Jeff uses the senior management monthly meeting as an opportunity to practice these steps:

Four STEP In-The-Moment Conversations Guidelines

1. Seize the Moment and Regain Focus

- Clear your mind from the background noise
- Expand **awareness** of the real challenge

2. Remember the Future and Craft a Shared Vision

- **Reflect** on possibilities for ideal conflict solutions
- Discover an energizing shared vision of possibilities

3. Learn from the Past to Build Organizational Alignment

- Inspire new **insights** from lessons learned
- Commit to alignment toward the shared vision

4. Seek Accountability to Champion Execution Habits

- Seek mutual trust, respect and accountability
- **Execute** new habits for accelerating growth momentum

Seize the Moment and Regain Focus

At times, during the Senior Management meeting, Jeff understands the need to be like a coach calling time-out from an intense, competitive game of business.

Even though this is a scheduled meeting, he considers it a special moment in time that will impact the lives of hundreds of employees and thousands of residents. Also, he knows the decisions being made will accelerate or decelerate the momentum of HKP's business growth.

The atmosphere of the meeting is similar to a professional sports team, sitting on the bench, regaining focus and energy. Imagine your favorite professional basketball team sitting on the bench to rest, drinking some water or Gatorade and relishing the chance to regain focus on the realities of the game being played. *What's the score? How are we as a team?*

Instead of drinking Gatorade though, most of Jeff's team are drinking coffee!

Even though each VP is extremely busy, and there are thousands of interactions and decisions being made during the two hours of their meeting, each VP gives a report about the realities they are facing with calmness, poise and candor.

Jeff knows the value of creating an atmosphere of calmness and mindfulness, even when there are some messy issues with turnover, financial underperformance at the properties, construction delays because of bad weather, complications or closings on new properties and the ever-challenging issue of cash flow.

Each VP demonstrates and models mutual trust, respect and accountability. Even though it becomes tense, no one holds back to celebrate victories, or acknowledge the brutal facts of loss.

Remember the Future and Craft a Shared Vision

Like the coach of a professional basketball team who grabs a clipboard to design the play, Jeff references the one-page strategic game plan to confirm the shared vision.

He understands how easy it is to be gripped by the tactics of the day, and he uses these precious few moments with his Senior Management team to remember the future vision. It is very energizing!

Twice a year, Jeff and the Senior Management team get off the grid and retreat for two days to craft a shared vision of greatness. The game plan that they develop continues to guide decisions in conversations daily, weekly, monthly and quarterly whenever the VPs meet.

Leaders use this Four STEP Model for improving a scheduled meeting, or for a brief one-on-one conversation with a fellow colleague. Remembering the future removes any personal attack when engaged in evaluating productive conflict solutions.

Learn from the Past to Build Organizational Alignment

When there is a gap between what is ideal and the realities being faced, it's important to have a growth mind-set. The concept of a growth mind-set is that life is never perfect, and that we can learn from failure and mistakes.

Jeff always remembers to ask, "What did we learn from our failures, and from our successes?"

Jeff models the ideas shared in Daniel Coyle's *The Culture Code*. He replicates how Navy SEALs conduct post-military-operations and have what is called an AAR: After Action Review.[34]

Each of the VPs feels psychologically safe enough to be open about failures and successes. To a person, they check their ego at the door.

Typically, during this phase of the conversation, a plan begins to emerge and is developed. They choose who will do what, by when, to fill the gap between the ideal future vision and the realities being faced. Then, the VPs remember that after they have vulnerability-based trust and productive conflict solutions, they promise to commit to the plan.

They have learned from Patrick Lencioni, author of *The Five Dysfunctions of a Team*, how to put into practice the two phases of commitment. The first phase is to make sure everyone weighs in. Jeff is sure to ask everyone around the conference room table to share their opinion on the challenges and decisions being made.

It's when those opinions differ from one another that innovative ideas often emerge. Like a good coach, Jeff encourages debate as people weigh in.

Often Jeff will wait for consensus. But there are many times when he just hears everyone out and then makes the decision.

It's at that point that everyone knows the second phase of commitment is to buy-in, even when their opinion or ideas did not lead to an action they wanted.

As a cohesive team, after the debate and constructive, dynamic friction, they are unified to go forward with the plan that has emerged.

It's at this point each VP who has assumed some accountability for follow-up and follow-through must be willing to ask for and receive accountability.

Seek Accountability to Champion Execution Habits

Jeff and his Senior Management team meet monthly with the key leaders from the culture who are committed to the habits necessary to achieve the shared vision.

The Rockefeller Habits Checklist from the Scaling Up Growth Tools starts with the first habit: the executive team is healthy and aligned.

Year by year, the Senior Management team continues to drive execution habits throughout the whole culture.

Each VP also models the discipline it takes to accelerate the momentum of the HKP business flywheel. They inspire every employee to seek accountability for the habits necessary to scale up.

Great! I have just shared with you how a business owner and a Senior Management team practice In-The-Moment Conversations for productive conflict solutions in team meetings.

In the next four chapters, you will encounter guidelines to prepare for and implement the Four STEPs along with the Eight Accelerator Questions Guide. These questions will help you apply this productive conflict solutions method to your organization and will inspire mindful leadership at every level.

"To make conflict productive, view it as a learning experience, not a contest. Emotionally intelligent leadership begins with staying clear about the overall objective of an organization or endeavor.

Keeping the focus on strategic goals prevents a conflict from shifting to damaging attacks on the individual.

Not only can this be beneficial to the relationships of all involved, but it also keeps the conversation on-topic, heading towards productive resolution."[35]

- Daniel Goleman

How Owners Stop Pussssshhhhhing!

A great example of a growth firm that understands the need for everyone in the culture to embrace productive conflict solutions as an essential leadership skill is the Cobblestone Homes team.

Mark and Melissa Wahl, entrepreneurs and co-founders, know what it feels like to start up a business. From the beginning, they pushed the heavy flywheel of breaking into the Michigan luxury home building business in Bay City and Saginaw. They have been pushing, year by year, turning that flywheel.

Even though they are now staffed with 18 employees and have an on-demand team of dozens of subcontractors, Mark and Melissa are conditioned, after years of doing it themselves, to continue *pussssshhhhhing* the flywheel themselves!

They are often gripped by the need to take corrective action when things start veering off course. They get involved when off schedule. They are sucked into daily operations to put out some "fire." Or you could say, they get involved when their business becomes like a "leaky bucket"[36] through inefficient or ineffective systems and processes. C players, client frustrations and time wasters can also cost millions, according to Howard Shore, best-selling author of *Your Business is a Leaky Bucket*.[37] The important thing is that In-The-Moment Conversations must be effective.

But just as important, these conversations have to take place. They can't be put off just because they could be unpleasant.

Despite what we might hope, otherwise known as "hopium," most problems don't just go away.

Right Moments

Bringing up unpleasant issues requires a scaling up culture where everyone feels safe to engage everyone else.

When everyone holds everyone else accountable, it's a culture that works. You don't have to think about it. You respond because "that is what we do here."

This culture of accountability to practice productive conflict solutions is especially critical when a company is scaling up.

The usual barrier to effective growth is a lack of leadership throughout an organization.

But don't misunderstand. Everyone in a company can be, and should be, developing their leadership skills.

What many people do not realize is that the key leaders in a business—the owner, the executives, the senior staff—are not actually in charge. It is their function to "take care of those in their charge," as was said by Simon Sinek!

The job of the designated leaders is to share the big picture, protect the corporate culture, maintain standards, close the big deals and deal with government regulations. It is not the everyday daily operations, the minutiae that all companies confront.

Not all In-The-Moment Conversations need to, or should, be held on the spot within sight and sound of colleagues, clients and customers. But in some cases, that is quite appropriate.

A problem which can be dealt with in a whisper is a problem which is easy to solve and does not have to be escalated. Escalation—asking for a closed-door meeting—can give the impression of seriousness and cause stress and anxiety, all of which, without exception, can be destructive and counterproductive.

All In-The-Moment Conversations need to be productive, whether they deal with situations that need to be dealt with in the present moment or scheduled, as the case may be, depending on the topic and who needs to be present.

That is why I shared the example of Jeff Kittle. He will practice productive conflict solutions, "In-the-Moment," in weekly strategy sessions, monthly meetings and during one-on-one meetings.

Reframing Conflict

While Peter Drucker writes that a leader is anyone with followers, Brené Brown teaches us in *Dare to Lead* that leadership is influence and anyone that has influence is a leader.[38]

A fundamental principle is that you must accept self-leadership because if you do not hold yourself accountable, you can't hold anyone else accountable for their actions. And by the way, inaction is also an action.

Reframing friction into productive conflict solutions is an essential leadership competency. Often, when people hear the word "conflict," they react negatively because they don't want to have conflict. That's a natural reaction. No one wants to have conflict because it leads to drama. No business wants drama.

That is why it is so important that we reframe **"conflict."** We use the definition from the Productive Conflict Profile as simply **"a difference of opinion."** Tension is inevitable, but it should be viewed like the weights on a scale. If you avoid tension, one side of the scale will tip over, and that will be unproductive.

Create a culture where it becomes the new normal to reframe the realities of friction, confusion and underperformance without undo threat. Be energized by a shared vision. Get back into alignment to make the changes necessary to seek accountability. That means everyone will admit to their errors, face the realities as they are, ask for help and be encouraged to achieve their next level of best.

Create a culture that seeks mutual trust, respect and accountability.

It starts with each person seeking accountability.

This has to be the new normal.

Learn to be more comfortable, being uncomfortable.

The rest of this book is designed to make it easier to have the harder conversations when there are differences of opinion. This may include personality conflicts, miscommunications between teams, differing priorities, perceptions that others are not carrying their load, frustrations with others for not following up, too much work, pressure to hit the numbers, etc.

Dr. Daniel Goleman, the author famous for studying Emotional Intelligence, said this:

> **The states of disengagement are epidemic in some workplaces. The experience of too much stress, called frazzle, is also epidemic. Both disengagement and frazzle disable the brain's prefrontal zones, the site in the brain of comprehension, focus, learning and creativity.**
>
> **On the other hand, in the zone for flow, the brain operates at peak cognitive efficiency, and people perform at their best.**
>
> **This redefines the essential task of the Leader: to help people get and stay in the brain zone where they can work at their best. Effective leaders create a resonance with those they lead and neural harmony that facilitates flow.[39]**

When you put this knowledge into practice, you can transform…

- friction into productive conflict,

- confusion into clarity, and

- underperformance into accelerating the momentum of business growth.

Part 3

**Preparing for
In-The-Moment
Conversations
Productive Conflict
Solutions**

The Defining Moments

In the book *The Power of Moments*, Chip and Dan Heath teach us this from their research:

> A defining moment is a short experience that is both memorable and meaningful. Why would you want to create them? To enrich your life. To connect with others. To make memories. To improve the experience of customers or patients or employees. Our lives are measured in moments, and defining moments are the ones that endure in our memories.[40]

What do we mean by using the phrase *seize the moment?*

A remarkable story of seizing the moment—a "defining moment" at the right time—comes from news reporter Zak Keefer, Indianapolis Colts insider. Zak wrote the story of a remarkable turnaround of the Indianapolis Colts who had been underperforming during the 2018 season.[41]

He told the story about Jacoby Brissett, backup quarterback, who texted a few teammates in mid-October 2018, just after the team's 1–4 win-loss record became 1–5. Keefer wrote:

> 'What do you think?' [Brissett] asked one veteran. 'Should we all meet?'
>
> They let the idea marinate for a few days, then decided: Enough was enough. It was time.

It was mid-October. The Indianapolis Colts weren't the worst team in football, but their record argued otherwise: They sat at the bottom of the AFC and were tied with the Arizona Cardinals for the worst record in the league.

The losses were piling up, and so were the frustrations.[42]

The whole team knew that this was the time to *seize the moment.* They chose to seek accountability and demonstrate the leadership required to address what Drucker said is natural for all organizations: "friction, confusion and underperformance."

This was the moment in their season to *regain focus.* This was the moment for teammates to look eye-to-eye. Brissett's leadership influenced everyone to acknowledge the hard truth and the realities of the team's underperformance.

More than likely, your employees will not gather on their own to have such a meeting to address the friction, confusion and underperformance.

That's why Chris Ballard, General Manager for the Indianapolis Colts, knows how important culture is to a winning organization and said so on day one:

> …we want high-character guys that love football, that will hold each other accountable, that will be good teammates. Look at the teams that win in this league. It's culture. Culture wins. It absolutely wins.[43]

Defining Moments for Your Organization

What are the defining moments before it becomes a crisis and decreases the momentum of your business flywheel? Let's see an example.

This is a list of defining moments generated by the Cobblestone Homes team during their training for Productive Conflict Solutions:

- Unexpected changes

- Unreasonable expectations

- Dirty jobsite by vendors

- "No call, no show" by vendors

- Lack of attention to detail

- Failure to use a checklist

- Uncooperative attitude

- Lack of a sense of urgency

- Failure to do their part

- Destructive conflict

- Avoidance of conflict

Take a few minutes now, individually or with your team, to brainstorm moments—defining moments—that accelerate or decelerate the momentum of your business growth, your flywheel.

Write your defining moments here:

Our defining moments:

_____

_____

_____

_____

_____

_____

_____

_____

_____

Great! You have a list of defining moments that warrant In-The-Moment Conversations. We will use this later when you design your In-The-Moment Conversation.

Behavioral Styles Impact

Next, consider how you can learn to accelerate thru conflict more effectively and efficiently. Become self-aware of the impact of your behavioral style during conflict. Learn to adapt your behavioral style to the behavioral styles of your colleagues.

In her best-selling book, *Dare to Lead*, Brené Brown says this about self-awareness as the key to leadership:

> I define a leader as anyone who takes responsibility for finding the potential in people and processes and who has the courage to develop that potential. We desperately need more leaders who are committed to courageous wholehearted leadership and who are self-aware enough to lead from their hearts, rather than evolved leaders who lead from hurt and fear.[44]

That means an assessment is in order to gain self-awareness, just so we don't miss something because of our own blind spots. An assessment that would advise you on how to adjust to the styles of others during conflict is crucial.

Assessing Productive Conflict

We recommend the Productive Conflict Profile by John Wiley & Sons, Inc. for a refreshing, new assessment.[45]

When you receive your profile, you will gain self-awareness, and empathy for those with whom you engage. Also, you will learn about the preferences, stressors and possible destructive tendencies during conflict for yourself and others. It is very important to discover how to be mindful of your strengths and blind spots.

Those who participate in this profile will contribute to creating a climate where it's psychologically safe enough to embrace conflict and to make sure it is productive.

Everyone struggles with conflict at work to varying degrees. Every day at work, it's natural to navigate a workplace with competing interests and clashing personality styles, with limited time and resources.

Hopefully, you share the same goals as your colleagues, but you don't always agree on how to achieve them.

We all work differently. We can irritate each other and become frustrated. We sometimes get caught up in the politics of jockeying for position. But natural disagreements should be welcomed and don't have to necessarily be a source of unhealthy conflict.

A Brief Behavioral Styles Tutorial

Even if you don't have Wiley's Profile or want to use that tool, I recommend that you take a moment to consider the priorities of your style and the styles of your colleagues when facing conflict.

Here is a quick tutorial!

DISC stands for....

Dominant
Influence
Steadiness
Conscientious

Possible priorities during conflict for each style:

D—getting to the point; controlling conversations; winning

I—speaking up; seeking reassurance; being optimistic

S—listening; smoothing over things; restoring stability

C—sticking to the facts; critical thinking; conceding even if you don't think you are wrong

From this list of priorities, what is your primary natural style? Of course, you can have a blend of styles; however, choosing your primary natural style is helpful to understand the impact of your style on others.

What is your primary natural style and the primary style of a colleague with whom you will be preparing to engage in productive conflict solutions? Give this your best shot!

This example will show you why this is important.

Sam and Susie are colleagues working together to finish a project. Sam asks to speak with Susie because they were behind schedule early in the project. He requested an In-the-Moment Conversation with Susie. Using the method described, Sam acknowledged that he was primarily interested in the priorities of the "D" style. He knew that he tended to be controlling. The positive impact is taking charge and getting things done. The negative impact made it hard for him to work on a team because he would tend to dominate.

Sam recognized that Susie's priorities were more in line with the "S" style. The positive impact of her style was her ability to seek harmony with others and desire stability. The negative impact of her style was that she would not typically speak up, for fear of disrupting relationships with others.

With this knowledge, Sam decided to adapt his style, listen to learn the roadblocks that were blocking Susie from staying on track with the deadlines.

He also recognized that he needed to work with her to give more autonomy of choice and not control the conversation. He chose to make it safe for her to speak up and gain commitment to stay on schedule.

Now it's your turn. Using our example, plan how you will show up with a colleague during a defining moment to engage in productive conflict solutions:

Acknowledge my style_____

Acknowledge my colleague's style_____

Ok, great. Now, what I want you to consider are your priorities during conflict. This can be very helpful as you prepare for In-The-Moment Conversations.

Choose the priority that is most important for you during conflict:

_____

What is the positive impact of your priority during conflict?

_____

What is the negative impact of your priority during conflict?

_____

Now choose the priority that is most important for a colleague during conflict:

_____

What is a positive impact on you from your colleague's priority during conflict?

_____

What is a negative impact on you from your colleague's priority during conflict?

_____

Thanks for doing this exercise.

We will use this information when you do an exercise to prepare for STEP 1 of the In-The-Moment Conversations process. If you want to improve your ability to put into practice productive conflict solutions, this information will improve your ability to "seek first to understand, then to be understood.®"[46]

Why Focus on Conflict?

When working with a team to debrief the Productive Conflict Report, one teammate asked, "Why are we discussing conflict at work? We don't have conflict. Conflict is a word used to describe aggression. Conflict is when I have an argument with my spouse."

Another colleague said, "We do have some friction and have differences of opinion, but we usually avoid conflict because we think conflict could damage our relationships." A third teammate chimed in and said, "If we keep avoiding conflict, we will miss opportunities to innovate and improve our products and services."

When I coached this team, I helped them confront the notion, held by most people, that **conflict is a word to describe aggression and is always negative.**

Conflict at work is not as severe as we typically understand that word.

For the purpose of this book and our training, we define conflict as a difference of opinion, misalignments and disagreement that naturally occur from friction, confusion and underperformance, which are all natural for growth firms.

Our definition is based on the reality that people are inherently different, and conflict simply happens when those differences come to light. Viewing conflict in this way can help you maximize the possible positive outcomes of problems at

hand that need solutions. **Learning how to handle conflict is what matters.**

Are In-The-Moment Conversations Really Coaching Conversations?

In 1999, I was trained by Ron and Carol Ernst in their incredibly effective *RealTime Coaching* model.[47]

I learned from Ron and Carol that great coaches evoke insights through coaching questions and summarizing often what the coachee says. This coaching dialogue leads to changes of thinking within the coachee that lead to improved performance in the workplace.

Rarely do professional business or executive coaches interject their opinions or suggestions for that change.

A professional coach is focused on generating insights within the coachee and does not engage in debate nor into intentional productive conflict.

Executive leaders/managers should be trained and certified in coaching and stop micro-managing. When an executive leader or manager is in the position of a coach, it is less threatening for a direct report to learn to be a coachee.

When colleagues designate one person as the coach and the other person as the coachee, they need to be well-trained in that dynamic.

In-The-Moment Conversations are all about two or more people who can equally share opinions, **and even debate, but will do so productively.**

However, in this model, the dialogue stimulates awareness, reflection, insights and actions.

That requires a desire for self-leadership and self-coaching.

What do we mean by that?

90% Of Coaching Is Self-Coaching

Seth Godin, best-selling author and blogger, wrote a post titled "90% of coaching is self-coaching."[48]

Toward the end of the post, he wrote:

> It's entirely possible to coach yourself. To develop internal habits and standards that help you ratchet forward, drip by drip. But when you find yourself alone in a "co" working space, or isolated from good leadership, or wondering about what's next, it might just be a signal that you're missing the 10% from the core, the seed that you can build on and then internalize.
>
> Sooner or later, all motivation is self-motivation. And the challenge and opportunity is in finding the external forces that will soon become internal ones.[49]

Listen-Learn-Ask-Empower

In-The-Moment Conversations use the Listen-Learn-Ask-Empower methodology, but it is still designed for equal sharing with each person speaking up.

It is also designed to create a safe space for active listening that will lead to insights about how to engage in productive conflict solutions.

To gain the perspectives of everyone on the team is not just a good idea, it is an operational necessity!

Creating a partnering climate where everyone assumes mutual trust and respect and where each person seeks accountability for achieving results and averting danger is crucial.

At the heart of the In-The-Moment Conversations is the *coach-like* style of leadership and the four components *Listen-Learn-Ask-Empower*, which together foster a climate where organizations keep getting better together.

In-The-Moment Conversations productive conflict solutions is effective by helping leaders do the following:

- Learn to honor the perspective of each team member, even when they differ;

- Communicate openly and candidly without fear of retribution;

- Ask for and offer feedback (or even better, feedforward); and

- Listen to and say the hard things that have to be addressed!

Two Essential Skills

Throughout history, there are incredibly disappointing stories of teams that should have held one another accountable but did not! The results can be devastating.

For example, the Space Shuttle Challenger tragedy resulted from a culture that discounted perspectives that challenged the status quo.

On the other hand, there are countless examples of partnering climates where everyone is encouraged to speak up and they are willing to seek accountability for results, safety and quality.

For example, in a hospital unit that fostered a partnering climate, an employee from housekeeping heard a sound in a patient's room that was an unusual cough.

Rather than thinking *It's not my job*, she opened the door to find a patient recovering from throat surgery choking on a cracker. Her effort saved that patient's life! That is a great example of mindful leadership at every level!

Consider the following two tips to better understand what it may take for you and your teammates to become more effective at In-The-Moment Conversations.

#1 Listen to Learn the Perspectives of Others

In the book *The 7 Habits of Highly Effective People* by Stephen Covey, we learn one of the most important habits for listening: **"Seek first to understand, then to be understood.®"**[50]

When you can summarize or paraphrase after reflecting on the words you've heard, you'll be more likely to understand and confirm that understanding with others.

When engaged in productive conflict solutions, we do not think **"for others"** and make judgments when listening. Rather, you are listening to guide your colleague to **think better and make better decisions through self-evaluation and self-coaching.**

Do you have a reputation for being willing to hear and speak the hard things? When listening, reflect on the brutal facts. However, it is also important to speak with candor and directness and don't dance around issues.

Go out of your way to seek the views of others on your team, especially those who may offer some insights to the challenges your team is facing.

Learn the perspectives, challenges and even limiting beliefs of your colleagues that may be blocking them from future growth.

Be sure to utilize what I call the "yes, and" approach. The "yes" is summarizing what you are learning about the other person's perspective. The "and" is your interest to learn more. It is great to follow up with

"And what else?"[51]

In the end, building a relationship of trust by offering and seeking open discussion creates a communication pathway that drives real impact. The impact is the ability to accelerate the momentum of business growth.

2 Ask Questions to Empower Others to Think

Ask open-ended questions that empower others to think and decide what it will take to achieve their next level of best.

Let's distinguish between closed versus open-ended questions. Closed questions extract information but precludes further discussion.

For example, we could ask, "May I help you?" The answer will be "Yes" or "No." The question, "How may I help you?" is an open-ended question that creates a more conversational tone.

When engaged with In-The-Moment Conversations, we have to be careful to eliminate the sense of interrogation that usually follows a series of closed questions.

It takes more effort to come up with open-ended questions as well as to pay close attention to the responses. I will share examples later in the book.

This can lead to greater participation in the exchange of ideas and can motivate someone to achieve a performance goal or a shared organizational goal.

Empathy can be the first step of influencing others to achieve their next level of best. They will learn to go beyond the "have-to" approach of providing value-creating service to a "want-to, self-motivated" approach of doing more than is expected.

Coach K: How to Listen-Learn-Ask-Empower

Take for example Mike Krzyzewski, aka "Coach K," the head basketball coach of Duke University's Blue Devils. In a career than spans nearly 40 years of coaching, he has more wins than any other NCAA basketball coach in history (as well as three Olympic gold medals as head coach of the USA Basketball Men's National Team).

Bret Stetka, in a *Scientific American Mind* article on Coach K, wrote the following:

> He has attributed his success, at least in part, to an epiphany he had while observing his family at the dinner table. [...] he noticed how his wife, Mickie, and their 3 daughters engaged with one another; how each showed interest in the others' day; how in tune they were with one another's feelings and the feelings of others. [Coach K] gradually

developed a coaching philosophy and style built on solidifying his relationships with players and listening to them.[52]

A note to owners, executive leadership teams and managers:

This starts with you.

Part 4

Mastering Productive Conflict Solutions

"Peace is not absence of conflict; it is the ability to handle conflict by peaceful means."[53]

-Ronald Reagan

STEP 1

Seize the Moment and Regain Focus

Clear Your Mind from the Background Noise

Expand <u>Awareness</u> of the Real Challenge

Before You Start

In your own mind, you may recognize that there is some misalignment with a project or some unmet expectations. You may have a challenge with your team or a feeling of frustration with one of your colleagues. It is not a crisis, but if ignored, it could fester and become a bigger issue in the future.

Before you approach the other person in order to address your concern through productive conflict, ask yourself the following questions.

Seize the Moment Preparation:

- ✓ What are the priorities during conflict that each person values, based on styles?

- ✓ What drains energy for each person during conflict?

- ✓ When is the best time to approach them?

- ✓ What will you do to turn down the background noise?

- ✓ Why is this moment the right moment?

- ✓ What's the outcome you desire?

- ✓ What is the best way to broach your concern; what will you say?

- ✓ Have you confirmed the reality that you are facing that must be addressed?

Seize the Moment Examples

You may have been putting off addressing your issue, hoping that it will get better on its own or go away.

As a result, you may have experienced energy drain and unproductive conflict due to "friction, confusion, and underperformance."

Decide the best time for you to seize the moment and face the reality of the situation you need to address.

Choose one of these four examples, just to get things started.

Example 1

"Hello_____, do you have a moment?

"I wanted to know if we could meet, either now or later, to address a concern I have about (name the concern)?

"It should only take about five or ten minutes. It's important for me to address this concern because (state reason). Why is this concern important for you?"

(Summarize what they say, thank them, and confirm the reality that you are going to address together.)

Example 2

"Hey_____, I have a challenge about

_____(name the challenge).

"Is this a good time or can we schedule five or ten minutes of uninterrupted time to focus on this issue?

"It's important to me to address this issue because
_____(state reason). Why is this concern important for you?" (Summarize what they say, thank them, and confirm the reality that you are going to address together.)

Example 3

"Hi_____, I would like to talk with you about _____ (name the issue).

"I need your help and wanted to know if this is a good time to spend ten minutes to address the issue and get things back on track?

"This issue is important to me because _____ (state reason). Why is this an important issue for you as well?" (Summarize what they say, thank them, and confirm the reality that you are going to address together.)

Example 4

"Hi_____, do you have a minute?

"I am frustrated about_____(name the frustration), and I have a personal concern about us working this out. Would it be okay to take five to ten minutes now to focus on this?

"This issue is important to me because_____ (name the issue). Why is this issue important for you as well?" (Summarize what they say, thank them, and confirm the reality that you are going to address together.)

Regain Focus

Great! You have seized the moment! Now let's regain focus!

The ability to regain focus, amidst a sea of distractions, is the key to a successful conversation.

Daniel Goleman, author of *Focus: The Hidden Driver of Excellence*, helps us understand that there is more than one type of focus:

> It takes insightful self-awareness and strong skills in self-management to attend to our inner territory, the emotional worlds of others, and what is going on in the larger systems of which we are a part. If your work includes giving feedback, motivating people and responding to changing situations in your environment, you need inner focus, focus on others and a focus on the world around you.[54]

Dr. Goleman makes this even more poignant. If you lack inner focus, you are "rudderless;" if you lack other focus, you are "clueless;" if you lack outer focus, you will get "blindsided."[55]

Clear Your Mind from the Background Noise

Now imagine, you are sitting in a room with a colleague. This could also be with a team, but let's just practice having an In-The-Moment Conversation with a colleague.

There is often anxiety when addressing conflict. You will need to address this whenever you have this conversation.

Perhaps this will help.

When I was trained by the NeuroLeadership Institute in a course titled Brain-Based Conversations, I learned a simple technique called "clearing the space."[56]

The idea is for each person to create mental, emotional and physical "space" from the sea of distractions and to be focused.

Imagine a popular waterskiing lake at noon on July 4th. Chaos! Lots of waves! If you throw a rock into the lake, there would be no ripples. They would get lost in the chaos.

Now imagine the same lake at 4 a.m. on July 5th. Calm! The surface is like glass. If you throw a tiny pebble, you can see ripples go on and on.

Like that, you need to create a climate where the thoughts, like the pebble on July 5th, can have a greater impact. It is vitally important for each of you to experience a calm space for awareness, reflection and insight that will lead to action!

Just like what Dr. Goleman suggests, it is essential for each person in the conversation to have a single-minded, inner focus, free from threat; an empathic focus on the other person's perceptions; and a focus on the needs of the organization and the marketplace.

When I train leaders to practice this, it's often

unfamiliar for them to check in with each other and to clear their minds of the background noise.

Our brains are overloaded with information as it is. It's like a computer that has too many programs open to operate effectively and efficiently.

When facing conflict, the "fight, flight or freeze" dynamics are automatically triggered. For conflict to be productive, we need to reduce that threat state.

Start the meeting to allow each person's brain to be in the moment and at ease to get the most value out of the conversation.

Each of you needs to answer this question:

"What's on your mind, that needs to be addressed, or put aside, to be fully present and focused?"

Each of you should take a moment, catch your breath and share your answer to that question. Then, each of you will simply say something like: **"I will put these thoughts and feelings aside to focus on our conversation."**

This practice is a very simple form of what is called "mindfulness."

Ari Weinzweig, cofounder of Zingerman's, understands this issue and how important it is for being fully present and engaged in all aspects of our lives.

In his pamphlet, "Secret #33 - Mindfulness Matters," he wrote this:

> In his book, *Man's Search for Meaning*, Victor Frankl writes, 'Between stimulus and response, there is a space. In that space lies our freedom and power to choose our response. In our response lies our growth and freedom.' To me, mindfulness is about actively moving into and spending as much time as possible—living, breathing, feeling, thinking and sensing—in that space. Ari continues and says, *"Choosing mindfulness is a conscious move towards self-growth and freedom, better leadership and a better life."*[57]

Starting the conversation with this simple practice sets the tone for the next phase.

Expand <u>Awareness</u> of the Real Challenge

There are three disciplines essential for In-The-Moment Conversations that will help you understand how to frame these conversations: priorities, data and meeting rhythms.

Remember, In-The-Moment Conversations need to take place, otherwise leaving issues unaddressed will negatively impact the momentum for scaling up.

Priorities: In-The-Moment Conversations help you to regain focus on the main thing, the most important priority. Individuals or organizations with too many priorities have no priorities and risk spinning their wheels and accomplishing nothing of significance.

In turn, laser focusing everyone on a single priority—today, this week, this quarter, this year and the next decade—creates clarity and power throughout the organization.

Data: In-The-Moment Conversations help to regain focus on what you learn from the data. It's like a sports team in a huddle during an important game. They need to stop playing the game, catch their breath, and look at the data, the brutal facts and realities.

As it relates to your business, are you following your game plan? What's the score? How much time do you have to accomplish your goal?

Meeting Rhythms: In-the-Moment Conversations will help you:

- regain focus through candid productive conflict solutions;

- bring disagreement out in the open;

- help de-escalate conflicts;

- focus on issues, not personality conflicts; and

- celebrate collective results and exceptional effort by your teammates.

Engagement and performance at work result in large part from the hundreds of daily interactions and conversations you have, whether with direct reports, supervisors, colleagues or customers.

Business Example of Conflict

A common issue for commercial real estate firms around the country comes up when the owner or business development team seizes the moment in the marketplace to buy properties of high value at a good price.

Often, owners will bring in the talent to make a judgment call on whether or not to buy a property. They will hire highly skilled analysts to guide the decisions to buy or sell properties in cities beyond the range where they normally work.

In one quarter, when the market is right, owners may purchase multiple new properties as they scale up. To manage the new property, the employee count goes up quickly. This can create a lot of stress and often meets the criteria described by Dr. Goleman earlier of being frazzled.

During one of my coaching sessions, an owner said, "Look at these numbers!" The occupancy for all the new assets had dropped below the percentages expected in the pro forma.

"I need some coaching to understand my role as the owner to help the deal guys work better with the management teams who are trying to keep up with the pace of change."

Reframing Automatic Thoughts

When I was working with the owner during her one-on-one coaching session, she was seeing data that showed the majority of the properties were performing according to the pro forma. What kept getting the owner and the finance team's attention were the new properties that were behind in achieving their goals.

I asked her, "What do you think when you look at the numbers of the underperforming properties?"

"I'm thinking the property management team is not doing their job!" she exclaimed. "We have pressure to report back to our investors, and the pressure really mounts."

Then I asked her, "When you are with the finance team and you all begin to think that property management is not doing their job, what happens then?"

"We start thinking of interventions," she said, "because we're convinced that they're not doing their jobs! So, we want to fix it!"

"Is it actually true" I asked, "to think they're not doing their jobs? Is there any other way for you and the finance team to think about why these numbers don't match the proforma?"

"Dr. O," she confessed, "as we revealed in previous coaching sessions, when threatened, my automatic thoughts take over. I interpret the numbers negatively and assume the worst."

"And when you make this judgment call," I said, "you set an emotional climate for your finance team to be at odds with the property management team.

"I use the acronym CRAP as a reminder of how important it is for an owner to model critical thinking skills for all leaders in the organization.

"Mindful leaders have the capacity and insight to observe data as just news. Usually, automatic thoughts bypass critical thinking and lead to false interpretations of the news as 'bad' or 'good.'

"Let's put into practice critical thinking skills to better interpret the data and stop making assumptions and biases that can lead to destructive conflict."

Then, I wrote this on the board:

> **Challenge assumptions**
>
> **Root out biases**
>
> **Ask questions that draw out new alternatives**
>
> **Press for evidence to support new solutions**

Critical Thinking

Mike Evans and the team at CHORUS Inc. developed a remarkable assessment called Hallmarks of Excellence® in Leadership.[58]

What I wrote on the board is a way of understanding Critical Thinking and how it is an important attribute measured by the Hallmarks of Excellence in Leadership assessment.

When we practice critical thinking, we can linger with ambiguity. Lingering with ambiguities is a crucial skill for leaders. Why? Because then you can focus on solutions rather than just problem solving using old ways of thinking.

Back to my conversation with the owner.

"For many business owners like yourself," I noted, "lingering with ambiguity just doesn't seem right!"

The owner responded, "Well, my team seeks the opposite of ambiguity. We jump into problem-solving right away."

When you take this first step of In-The-Moment Conversations, take a moment to pause, to nonjudgmentally observe the reality at hand. Otherwise, assumptions and biases take over your decision-making process.

"What were the assumptions and biases you were making about the property management division?" I asked. "How do assumptions and biases impact clarity in decision making?"

The owner responded quickly by saying, "We assumed they weren't doing their job! And because they weren't doing their job, our finance team began to come up with some actions to solve the problems!"

Then I asked, "What was the response from the director of property management?"

"She defended her team and their approach," she said. "She felt the finance team was getting out of their own swim lanes."

It was at this point that the owner and I pulled out the Productive Conflict Profile. We analyzed why this conversation became destructive.

The owner had a very direct style, and her automatic thoughts were influenced by her old assumptions and biases. This made it nearly impossible to avoid conflict with the Director of Property Management, who favored a more collaborative style and the ability to linger with ambiguity and think critically.

With the insights from the coaching session the owner decided to call a meeting with the finance and property management leaders. They began the meeting by asking the following questions to acknowledge assumptions and biases that led to destructive conflict between the teams.

"What is on your mind that you can set aside, to be present now, and be focused?"

"What is the conflict, and what is the real challenge for you?"

The owner was amazed at how these questions made it safer for everyone to be candid about their biases and assumptions.

After completing the **Four STEP** In-The-Moment Conversations productive conflict solutions process, each person on the team made a commitment to communicate directly and productively, as needed, to face conflict and to keep getting better together.

Case Study for STEP 1

I received a call from a business owner who wanted to prepare for an In-The-Moment Conversation with a key leader in his business. Here is the narrative. The names are fictitious, but the story is true. Scott is the owner. Charlie is accountable to develop budgets for new construction.

I will share this example to help you as a reader to understand STEP 1.

I answered the phone. "Hi Scott, how may I help you?"

"Hi Doc, I want to prepare for an In-The-Moment Conversation with Charlie."

I said, "Let's clear our minds of the background noise. What's on your mind that you could put aside to be present now, and focused?"

Scott shared he had some phone calls to make but had a clear mind and was happy to work with me.

I shared that I have nothing on my plate that would distract me. "I am a little tired from work today, but happy to help."

Scott said, "I appreciate the time. Ten minutes should work. I am relieved you have the time to help. Prior to this call, I was feeling frustrated."

"Scott," I said, "I just modeled for you the concept of clearing the space. Always make sure each person involved in the In-The-Moment Conversation takes a moment of pause to be present, regain focus and set aside the distractions."

"Thanks for modeling that," said Scott. "I hardly think to do anything like that. When there is conflict, I want to go right to the problem and figure out a solution. This would be a great practice. I see the value."

I said, "Do you remember the idea of **automatic thoughts** from the Productive Conflict Profile? Just to review, automatic thoughts are assumptions about the other person that come up in our head, like banner ads on your computer."

Then I asked, "Did you avoid speaking with Charlie? If so, what were the automatic thoughts?"

Scott said, "Yeah, 'I don't want to be seen as the bad guy.' But I am thinking, 'Why doesn't he get it, since we discussed this issue before?' I also thought, 'I really don't like it when I am not heard.'"

After summarizing his thoughts, something I do often in these collaborative conversations, I then asked, "What destructive behavior emerged?"

"Well," Scott said, "I just complained about it with the CFO and then we just fixed it!"

"Scott, what have you learned so far from our conversation?" I asked.

Scott said, "I have to clear the junk in my head, clear

my mind and reduce the emotion. Otherwise, I would go into a conflict meeting frustrated. Also, I realize I need to prepare for the conversation by using the In-The-Moment checklist you provided."

Now that we have cleared the space mentally, I asked Scott, **"What is the conflict?"**

"The conflict is with Charlie," he said. "When confronted, he always has an excuse and is blaming and defensive. He has a pattern of using previous budgets for new projects. Recently, when he did that, he made a mistake that cost us over $10,000."

After summarizing what Scott said, I asked him the next key question:

"What is the real challenge for you concerning this conflict you just described?"

Scott replied, "The loss of money is a concern. However, the real challenge is influencing Charlie to change his budgeting process because it slows down closings and doing other deals. Also, I want Charlie to recognize his pattern of making a mistake, having an excuse and blaming someone else. What I just described is in his profile."

"Scott," I prodded further, "what have you learned about getting started with **STEP 1**?"

Scott replied, "I typically don't clear the distractions before I get started. I can see that doing that will reduce the threat for me when giving feedback and for him receiving feedback!"

He continued, "It is very easy for me to just fix things and go on. It is stressful for me to be engaging in conflict, but this process makes it easier to do what seems so hard and uncomfortable!"

Then he finished by saying, "I also learned that it is possible to face the conflict, get right to the real challenge and keep it in the context of growing the business. The rest of the steps will flow more easily now."

I will share the rest of the story throughout the book as to how Scott and I had our own In-The-Moment Conversation in each **STEP**.

As a side note, when I followed up with Scott to see how our conversation impacted his conversation with Charlie, he said this:

"Doc, this stuff works!"

Now It's Your Turn!

Now, write down the conflict you want to address. What is the real challenge now? (For example, think of the impact on the customer, the team or the business growth momentum.)

_____

_____

_____

_____

_____

_____

_____

_____

_____

Whatever your position, an essential mindful leadership skill is to help those you work with get into and stay in the brain zone where they can work at their best and not get frazzled, especially when facing change!

When you embrace change through In-The-Moment Conversations, new connections in your brain are formed!

When you resist change, you are unable to make new connections. In that case, you can't think your way out of a problem, and you can become frazzled.

Don't get lost in the ocean of distraction that we all must navigate daily. **STEP 1** alleviates the problem of distraction and sets the tone for the rest of the conversation.

On the next page you will see the Eight Accelerator Questions Guide for the **FOUR STEP** In-The-Moment Conversations model. This guide allows you to get started with these conversations today. You will see this guide after each **STEP** is described.

Eight Accelerator Questions Guide

- Establish an agreement to meet at a certain time and place to give a few moments of undivided attention for increased awareness and insights.

- Practice "Listen to Learn; Ask to Empower" to make it safe for your colleague to speak up. Remember to summarize often by reflecting on what is being said.

- Each of you will ask these questions out loud for your colleague to answer candidly.

Seize the Moment and Regain Focus

1 - What's on your mind, that needs to be addressed, or put aside, to be fully present and focused?

2 - What is the conflict, and what is the real challenge for you?

Remember the Future and Craft a Shared Vision

3 - What is the ideal outcome, and what will it mean for you to achieve it?

4 - If we don't resolve this conflict, what will be the outcome, and what will it mean for you?

Learn from the Past and Build Organizational Alignment

5 - What insights have you learned during this conversation?

6 - What will you promise to do, by when, to be in alignment to achieve our shared vision?

Seek Accountability to Champion Execution Habits

7 - What are the "if, then" habits you will put into practice to keep the promises we just made?

8 - How and when will you seek accountability to verify you are in alignment?

STEP 2

Remember the Future and Craft a Shared Vision

<u>Reflect</u> on Possibilities for Ideal Conflict Solutions

Discover an Energizing Shared Vision of Possibilities

The Push to Get Results

In growth firms, there's a push to get results! Daily operations can get bogged down for a variety of reasons like staffing constraints, customer service problems and delivery issues, to name but a few.

If there's a customer service problem, or confusion on the team, it's a challenge to stay focused on the longer-term vision.

That requires what is called "visionary leadership," one that fosters a climate to craft a shared vision that everyone in your culture understands and embraces.[59]

In their January 2009 *Harvard Business Review* article, Jim Kouzes and Barry Posner wrote:

> **The only visions that take hold are shared visions—and you will create them only when you listen very, very closely to others, appreciate their hopes, and attend to their needs. The best leaders are able to bring their people into the future because they engage in the oldest form of research: They observe the human condition.[60]**

Remember the Future!

It is like climbing a mountain. To use a simple analogy, many people dream of summiting Mount Everest. Those mountain climbers who do it, and not just dream it, craft a shared vision with a team skilled in what it will take to climb a mountain such as Everest.

In the end, it's about keeping everyone focused on the summit. The summit is a metaphor for your shared vision and mission.

When there is a scarcity of time, people and resources, it may be seen as an immediate threat. It's like a fire that must be put out! It's nearly impossible to remember the future vision or the shared long-term goal when putting out fires!

If your own organization's long-term strategies were developed by the owner, CEO and their strategic counsel, everyone would be expected to deliver the shared vision.

What Is Missing?

A vivid description of the future is missing!

Vivid is the difference between watching an old western on a black-and-white TV versus the same western at an IMAX theatre with 3D glasses.

When you remember the future, you will have the energy and willpower to overcome obstacles and challenges when scaling your Everest!

In-The-Moment Conversations improve the quality and participation in most meetings. They create a climate that keeps everyone engaged and focused in high-quality candid conversations aimed at crafting and achieving a shared vision.

When the executive leaders impose what they think the team ought to be, and it's not consistent with the team's shared vision of an ideal outcome, the leaders may be contributing to the team members feeling threatened, which may cause them to close their minds and willingness to change.

Crafting a shared vision is a positive, hopeful state that can inspire your teams. Do that and your teams will be healthier and more capable and more willing to do what it takes to scale up to your organization's summit.

This is the most neglected step. STEP 2 is all about magnetizing a team toward the goal!

Focus on Results

When your company is growing, you must stay focused on results. You can't get derailed by the everyday distractions that plague all businesses.

Focus is everything. You must keep your eye on your long-term goal.

This takes that "visionary leadership" previously mentioned, that shared vision that the entire culture understands and embraces. It's the same as climbing a mountain. Your goal is to reach the summit.

But the only way to conquer Everest is with a team skilled in leadership. You literally and figuratively must follow the person in front of you. You must trust them, and they have to trust you. Their life depends on you, and your life depends on them.

Remember what Kouzes and Posner said: "The best

leaders are able to bring their people into the future because they engage in the oldest form of research: They observe the human condition."

You will be tested by the distractions, those fires that break out that you are forced to extinguish.

To stay on track, you need what we discussed previously—In-The-Moment Conversations, those exchanges that set the standard for productive conflict solutions.

Input from everyone on what it takes to execute strategies, especially the frontline staff, is vital to overcoming obstacles and challenges when scaling your company's Everest!

Executives cannot impose a shared vision on the team. Everyone must be a stakeholder who feels their contribution is appreciated and that their voice is heard.

Great coaches are, above all, experts in motivation. They initiate improvement in the competence of the team by inspiring strong positive relationships among the teammates.

Sports psychologists know that despite the time-honored tradition of coaching like a drill sergeant, the disciplinarian style has shifted. When the team huddles with the coach, the best coaches no longer just get out the clipboard and bark out orders!

Crafting a Shared Vision

One of my favorite movies is the 1986 classic *Hoosiers* starring Gene Hackman.[61] It's based on a true story of how a small Indiana school in the 1950s won the high school state basketball championship by beating a major powerhouse school.

During the last scene, with nineteen seconds left in the game, the team is huddled around the coach played by Hackman, who says, "Listen up. Listen up. Here's what we're going to do. Jimmie, they are expecting you to take the last shot. So we're going to use you as a decoy. All right, let's go!"

But the team put their heads down, their energy dropped, and the coach says, "What's the matter with you guys?"

There was a long silence, and then Jimmie, their best player, says, "I'll make it." The coach pauses, looks into the eyes of his team, and says: "Okay, Buddy, you get the ball to Jimmie at the top of the key."

Clasping their hands together, the coach shouts, "Let's go! Go team!" Then they break from their huddle and the five players head out onto the floor for the final nineteen seconds of play.

A few moments later, just a moment before the game clock expired, the spectators roar when Jimmie hits the game-winning jump shot!

Beyond the Safety of Silence

1. Have you experienced telling your team a plan of change, and then noticed the energy drop?

2. What is it like to be in a work climate where it is okay to be like Jimmie and speak up?

3. What insights did you gain about yourself as you reflect on how the coach in *Hoosiers* responded to his team?

Every day, employees make decisions about whether to speak up and seek conflict or remain silent and avoid conflict. The problem is, in many organizations, the majority choose the safety of silence and avoid conflict.

Silence and avoidance deny the organization and its leaders of valuable information that could be used to make improvements.

It is crucial to create feedback cultures where ideas and suggestions are shared, employees are listened to and appropriate responses to feedback are given.

Now, let's consider your insights about what it takes to craft a shared vision that includes the voices of your teammates and motivates others to face change.

Perhaps this will help.

The Positive and Negative Emotional Attractors

One of the world's greatest experts in understanding the inspirational power of a shared vision is Dr. Richard Boyatzis. His research on physiology and brain patterns explains what he calls the Positive Emotional Attractor, or PEA.[62]

The PEA is the brain chemistry of being motivated to move toward the vision of change.

He also coined the term Negative Emotional Attractor, or NEA, which is the brain chemistry of a threat state of the resistance to change.

The PEA helps you function at your best. Research in neuroscience shows that a shared vision can create a state that enables you to be open to new ideas and feeling motivated to embrace change.

The NEA has the opposite effect. This can occur when a leader is seeking compliance from the team without contributing any effort to get buy-in from team members for a proposed change.[63]

In the movie *Hoosiers*, the coach at first evoked the NEA when he said, "Listen up. Listen up." in the team huddle. The coach wanted compliance when he gave his plan for change to his players.

But then he shifted from the NEA and evoked the PEA, by listening to the team, crafting a shared vision and having a dialogue that energized the team to achieve that vision!

Questions to evoke the PEA:

Let's imagine we have achieved our number one priority for this quarter. Describe in vivid detail what you will see, feel or experience.

How will we define success as a team, or as an organization?

What inherent strengths do we possess, individually or as a team, that will help us achieve our goals?

What are the critical issues we need to be working on in the immediate future to stay on track with achieving our longer-term goals?

What will it be like, feel like and look like when we achieve our next level of best?

Are You Invoking the Negative Emotional Attractor?

In the previous chapters, I contrasted two styles of communication:

Listen-to-learn/Ask-to-empower

vs.

Hear-to-fix/Tell-to-solve

Many leaders want to **give a vision through directions and commands instead of inspiring a vision.** They are well meaning, but this only works short-term.

Do any of these phrases sound like you?

"I focus on fixing."

When most of us try to help someone, we often get sucked into focusing on the things that need to be fixed.

In the process, we invoke the NEA and the body's stress response. In other words, one colleague is being pushed toward the vision but is not involved in owning the vision.

"I try to improve weaknesses."

The desire for fast action can easily evolve into a premature focus on weaknesses. The belief is that by working on weaknesses, you will have the most impact on the person who is trying to improve. But that arouses the NEA and stops the change process.

"I know what others need."

Instead of invoking a colleague's ideal solution to a achieve a shared vision—their dreams of a possible and desired future, a PEA—the overly directive leader invokes the colleague's NEA.

When this style of leadership is imposed and is not consistent with the colleague's vision, the colleague could contribute to closing the mind of another colleague and their willingness to change.

Life is more exciting when we consider new possibilities and pursue them using a PEA question.

Every day, employees make decisions about whether to speak up or remain silent.[64] The problem is that, in many organizations, the majority choose the safety of silence. This denies the organization and its leaders' valuable information that could be used to make improvements.

While there are ways to address the problem of employee voice, it is strongly recommended by the researchers that all leaders of the organization receive training and coaching on how to create feedback cultures where ideas and suggestions are shared, employees are listened to and appropriate responses to feedback are given.

What are your insights about what it takes to inspire a shared vision that includes the voices of teammates and that motivates others to face change?

Case Study for STEP 2

Let's go back to our story with Scott as he is preparing for the In-The-Moment Conversation with Charlie. Here I will use the In-The-Moment Conversation process with Scott about planning his In-The-Moment Conversation!

Let's go back to the dialogue. "Scott, thank you for engaging in this dialogue with me. I have been modeling for you how to practice **STEP 1** of In-The-Moment Conversations."

I continued: "The next step is to remember the future and craft a shared vision. This is perhaps the most neglected step in this process. As you learned from the course, there's a tendency to name a problem and go right to the solution."

Scott chimed in: "You got it, Doc. I remember you really nailed it when you said there's a difference between 'hear-to-fix/tell-to-solve and listen-to-learn/ask-to-empower.'"

He continued, "When you used that flywheel metaphor, it's like I'm always pushing the flywheel, and fixing it when it gets out of alignment."

Scott said, "Now I realize, we can't scale the business if Sally and I are the ones doing all the pushing and fixing for our company. We already work day and night. It's only getting worse as we scale."

I realized Scott was describing the Negative Emotional Attractor described by Dr. Boyatzis.

"Scott, take a moment and reflect on what you were saying. Describe in detail your negative vision of you and Sally, working day and night, and it only gets worse. Describe what you see and feel!"

Scott admits, "I look worn out and feel grumpy!"

I summarized what he said and let him linger for a moment with that feeling.

"Scott, imagine you are at a fork in the road where you can see into the future. Imagine seeing yourself old and grumpy at the end of the left-hand fork. Now, look down the right-hand path and see and feel a positive future. What do you see?"

I gave him a moment or two to reflect on the vision.

Then he said, "I usually have a difficult time visioning, but the contrast between the two visions made it easier to see myself energized, and happy."

After reinforcing his experience, I asked him, "What did you learn about in **STEP 2** to magnetize Charlie toward a vision he creates with you?"

"I learned I can't just give him a vision," said Scott. "We need to work together on a shared vision of me liberated to do deals, and him achieving his vision of success, doing an exceptional job at bidding, only if it means something personal for him."

"Scott, that is a great insight!" I said. "You have learned to craft a shared positive vision of the future ideal outcome and to contrast that with the negative vision of what to avoid. This creates personal meaning.

"When you impose what you think the team ought to be, and it's not consistent with the team's shared vision of an ideal outcome, you may be contributing to the team members feeling threatened, closing their minds and their willingness to change. Here are two simple questions that will help you during STEP 2."

What is the ideal outcome, and what does it mean for you?

If we don't resolve this conflict, what will be the outcome and what will it mean for you?

"Scott, you are discovering how to inspire your colleagues to see their goals come alive!"

Make Defined Goals Shined Goals

Scott's defined goal was to improve Charlie's work. Scott's "shined" goal was to be liberated to be free to do more deals!

Here are other examples of defined goals being shined:

- A team member's goal to be promoted to senior consultant would shine when they see themselves handing out a business card!

- The goal to feel energized daily is shined up as "every day feels like a Saturday morning!"

- The goals to expand business by 20 percent is a shined-up vision of 1,000 loyal customers worldwide!

As we stated earlier, crafting a shared vision creates a positive hopeful state. Using this process, you will inspire your teams and they will be more aligned to work toward their shared vision and become more productive.

Eight Accelerator Questions Guide

- Establish an agreement to meet at a certain time and place to give a few moments of undivided attention for increased awareness and insights.

- Practice "Listen to Learn; Ask to Empower" to make it safe for your colleague to speak up. Remember to summarize often by reflecting on what is being said.

- Each of you will ask these questions out loud for your colleague to answer candidly.

Seize the Moment and Regain Focus

> *1 - What's on your mind, that needs to be addressed, or put aside, to be fully present and focused?*

> *2 - What is the conflict, and what is the real challenge for you?*

Remember the Future and Craft a Shared Vision

> *3 - What is the ideal outcome, and what will it mean for you to achieve it?*

> *4 - If we don't resolve this conflict, what will be the outcome, and what will it mean for you?*

Learn from the Past and Build Organizational Alignment

> 5 - What insights have you learned during this conversation?

> 6 - What will you promise to do, by when, to be in alignment to achieve our shared vision?

Seek Accountability to Champion Execution Habits

> 7 - What are the "if, then" habits you will put into practice to keep the promises we just made?

> 8 - How and when will you seek accountability to verify you are in alignment?

STEP 3

Learn from the Past to Build Organizational Alignment

Inspire New <u>Insights</u> From Lessons Learned

Commit to Alignment toward the Shared Vision

"If you could get all the people in an organization rowing in the same direction, you could dominate any industry, in any market, against any competition, at any time."[65]

- Patrick Lencioni

Increasing Complexity and Conflict

The scale-up companies our Cultures That Work (CTW) team serves are experiencing the complexity of scaling up.

When we go on-site, there is excitement over amazing deals and lots of money coming and going. The people are typically upbeat and are in alignment with growing a business and making a difference with strong core values and a purpose.

However, we also see increasing conflict as our clients scale. As coaches, we deal with the complexity of humans trying to deal with constant change by learning the skill of productive conflict solutions.

Typically, on the surface, the teams can really crank out the work. Beneath the surface, they experience automatic thoughts about themselves and each other as everyone experiences the pressure to get more done, faster, cheaper, better.

Most growth companies struggle to get everyone in alignment, rowing in the same direction, to execute their strategic plans.

According to the research from *The Balanced Scorecard*, authors David Norton and Robert Kaplan note that 90 percent of organizations fail to execute their strategies successfully.[66]

It's Our Choice

Perhaps this quote by British author Phyllis Bottome best summarizes our work so far:

> **There are two ways of meeting difficulties:**
> **You alter the difficulties, or you alter**
> **yourself to meet them.**

In this chapter, we will focus on how to reframe our automatic thoughts, learn from both failures and successes and use productive conflict solutions to get back into alignment!

Now, let's make this chapter as easy as 1, 2, 3:

1. Conflicting opinions are an inevitable part of workplace relationships and can be productive. Your response to conflict situations, whether you avoid or seek conflict, is in your own control.

2. We sometimes respond destructively to conflict. Why? Just below the surface of the mind, automatic thoughts are being played out, which in turn trigger destructive responses.

3. You can change your response when you're engaged with another person. Choosing to respond to others through productive conflict is what high-performance organizations do to achieve shared goals.

This Can Be Tough

It takes training and practice to step back during a conflict, but it becomes easier if you first acknowledge your emotions and how they influence your judgment.

During conflict, your emotions can sometimes clutter perspective and your long-term best interests. Emotions during conflict fall into these two broad categories: fight or flight. First ask yourself, "How do my emotions influence my automatic thoughts?"

Then, after you reframe your automatic thoughts, ask yourself, "How does my new perspective lead away from unproductive conflict toward productive conflict?"

Frazzled!!!

Dr. Daniel Goleman from Harvard Business School discovered that about 50 percent or more of how employees perceive their organization's climate can be traced to the actions of the leader.[67]

But, what about the other 50 percent? What can employees and teams do to create a great climate, especially when they become "frazzled"?

In Amy Arnsten's *Science* article "The Biology of Being Frazzled," the term "frazzle" is described as the neural state of the brain in which the anxious emotional upsurges hamper the thinking part of the brain.[68]

When "frazzled," no one can concentrate or think clearly.

The negative emotions of frazzle are contagious and sweep through the workplace like the flu, hampering team performance.

What can employees do, through their own self-leadership, to accept the other 50 percent of the responsibility for the work climate and reduce frazzle?

I will answer that question with a story.

Inspire New Insights from Successes and Failures

I coached the finance department of a commercial real estate firm that had just completed the Productive Conflict Profile.

When I sat down to start the coaching session, each person looked weary, frazzled.

The team was pressured by the owner to push through complex paperwork and transactions to close deals, often when it was least convenient.

There was unrelenting pressure from deadlines looming for year-end reports, payroll and next year's budgets. The owner expected them to close deals, even if it was inconvenient. Often, they had to drop everything and just do it, and that led to being frazzled!

That's the climate of a fast-growth firm. Get the deals done. Plus, they really liked the owner! Still, they were frazzled.

Then, I asked them a challenging question: "What if you could cut your frazzle in half?"

They welcomed the challenge.

Conflict situations are threatening and feel personal, and our instinct is to protect ourselves. Therefore, we may react so quickly that we don't even notice our thoughts. But beneath the surface is a thought process playing out: a conflict event triggers an automatic, biased, self-limiting thought, which in turn triggers a destructive response.

For example, automatic thoughts such as *I'm not backing down* and *You don't get it, I'm obviously right* could lead to arguing, gossip and belittling.

I encouraged the team to observe their automatic thoughts triggered during conflict.

One teammate, Sandy, put it this way. "When our owner disrupts us and wants to push a deal through, my automatic thought is *He doesn't care that I am overwhelmed, and I'll never get caught up.*"

Then she said, "Wow, now I realize my destructive responses. Those unexpressed, automatic thoughts lead me to withdraw, brood privately or gossip about the workload."

For the first time, she smiled! She seemed relieved! This team discovered a truth for all of us.

The drama of conflict and disagreement takes place within our own mind. In other words, most of the conflict is within us, and our thoughts are at odds with each other!

We can do something about that! That's how to cut our frazzle in half!

Each person on the team did the exercise in the Productive Conflict Profile and reframed their automatic thoughts. In particular, Sandy reframed her thoughts to *Our leader cares and we will cover each other's back.*

Mark Divine, Commander, Navy Seal (Retired), said this about reframing automatic thoughts:

> "Everyone must say to themselves when facing conflict, **I must challenge the story driving my behavior.**"[69]

Got Your Back

The whole team loved the new reframed thoughts, and each of them made a commitment to practice de-escalating emotions during conflict. They renewed trust in the owner, who did create a safe atmosphere for anyone to speak up.

It was just that the owner was a seeker of conflict.

Everyone on this team avoided conflict. After this training, they made a commitment to speak up and to ask for help when overwhelmed, rather than doubling down on the stress coming from outside of them.

They cut their frazzle in half!

Comfortable Being Uncomfortable

In this book, you have learned that it's best to manage conflicts by drawing out all parties, understanding the different perspectives of others and then finding a common shared vision that everyone can endorse.

Mindful leaders address the conflict, acknowledge the feelings and views of all sides, and then redirect the energy toward the shared vision.

Leaders who generate an atmosphere of collegiality and are themselves models of respect, helpfulness and cooperation, get results. They draw others into active, enthusiastic commitment to the collective effort.

In Daniel Coyle's best-selling book, *The Culture Code*, we learn this:

> One misconception about highly successful cultures is that they are happy, lighthearted places. This is mostly not the case. They are energized and engaged, but at their core, members are oriented less around achieving happiness than around solving hard problems together.[70]

Highly successful cultures hold numerous In-The-Moment Conversations. There is high candor, honest feedback, and uncomfortable truth telling. This is especially true when the team needs to confront the gap between where the team is and where it ought to be. To confront this gap, it is crucial to give and receive feedback. What is the best way to do that?

Commit to Alignment Toward the Shared Vision

Coyle also referred to the following study:

A few years back, a team of psychologists from Stanford, Yale and Columbia asked middle school students to write an essay after which teachers provided different kinds of feedback. Researchers discovered one form of feedback that was so immensely impactful on student performance that they deemed it "magical feedback."[71]

The feedback was not complicated. In fact, it consists of one simple phrase:

I'm giving you these comments because I have **very high expectations and I know that you can reach them.**[72]

Coyle also said: "That's it. Just nineteen words. None of these words contain any information on how to improve. They are powerful because they deliver a burst of belonging cues. When you look more closely, the sentence contains three separate cues:

1. You are part of this group.

2. This group is special; we have high standards here.

3. I believe you can reach those standards."

These signals provide a clear message that lights up the unconscious brain where the automatic thoughts reside. Here is a safe place to give effort.

Creating a safe place to have candid, high-quality In-The-Moment Conversations will almost always require you and your teammates to learn how to be more comfortable with the discomfort of giving candid feedback.

Most misalignment begins in our head and in our hearts. When frazzled, our perceptions of ourselves and others can be distorted, negative or positive.

True Measure of Engagement

Frazzled colleagues become disengaged. So, it is vitally important to identify disengagement before it leads to costly turnover. Without identification and measurement, the hidden forces of disengagement lead to underperformance, which, inevitably, impacts the customer experience and bottom-line finance.

So, why is it important to identify and measure engagement, beyond gut check and a feeling, about how things are going for you and others in your firm?

Jack Welch, former CEO of GE who led their efforts to increase engagement and performance, said this about the vital statistics of running a business:

> **There are three key indicators that really work:** employee engagement, customer satisfaction, and cash flow. It goes without saying that no company, small or large, can win over the long run without energized employees who believe in the mission and understand how to achieve it. [73]

In the battle to achieve a winning culture through energized employees, employee engagement data is what you need to go beyond just guessing at the engagement level of your employees.

Measurable employee engagement insights can turn intuition into action and transform the hard work of scaling up a business into purposeful, passionate and meaningful work.

However, influencing performance through meaningful work depends on the validity and value of a single metric: the engagement score. By assigning one simple, easy-to-understand score, everyone in the company can begin to understand how engaged they really are.

One such tool was developed by a company called Emplify. Emplify is the employee engagement company that unlocks the potential of the strongest competitive differentiator—people.

Santiago Jaramillo, cofounder of Emplify, is a coauthor of the book *Agile Engagement*[74] and describes their methodology: Informed by science and psychometrics, Emplify is the first to fuse a software platform, agile process and "human strategists" into a proven employee engagement system—one that is focused on achieving iterative business transformation through simple, actionable and timely measurement. Its employee engagement solution provides employees with a platform to access company information and voice feedback to company executives.

Scaling firms now use the data from their Emplify score as rigorously as they do financial data.

Case Study for STEP 3

"Scott, **STEP 3** starts with lessons learned. What

insights have you learned from this conversation?"

Scott thought for a moment and said, "Most of my stress about having productive conflict with Charlie is inside of me! I liked the idea about *being comfortable with being uncomfortable.*"[75]

I responded, "Candidly, I too am mainly stressed by my own automatic negative thoughts."

Then, Scott said, "I need to let Charlie know my thoughts first, just to show we are in this together. Since most of our automatic thoughts are named in the Productive Conflict Profile, it would also be great to understand each other and start being candid with each other."

I summarized what he said, and then I reminded Scott, this is the time to create a who-does-what-by-when commitment.

"Scott," I asked, "what will you promise to do, by when, to improve your alignment with Charlie?"

"I will study my profile and reframe my negative thoughts," he said. "I will prepare my meeting with Charlie with a quieter, less judgmental mind."

"Scott, there are two key questions for **STEP 3.**"

> *What insights have you learned during this conversation?*
>
> *What will you promise to do, by when, to be in alignment to achieve our shared vision?*

As Dr. Gary Chapman wrote in his book *Everybody Wins:*

> **When people respond too quickly;
> they often respond to the wrong issue.
> Listening helps us focus on the heart of
> the conflict. When we listen, understand,
> and respect each other's ideas, we can
> then find a solution in which both of us
> are winners.**[76]

Eight Accelerator Questions Guide

- Establish an agreement to meet at a certain time and place to give a few moments of undivided attention for increased awareness and insights.

- Practice "Listen to Learn; Ask to Empower" to make it safe for your colleague to speak up. Remember to summarize often by reflecting on what is being said.

- Each of you will ask these questions out loud for your colleague to answer candidly.

Seize the Moment and Regain Focus

> *1 - What's on your mind, that needs to be addressed, or put aside, to be fully present and focused?*

> *2 - What is the conflict, and what is the real challenge for you?*

Remember the Future and Craft a Shared Vision

> *3 - What is the ideal outcome, and what will it mean for you to achieve it?*

> *4 - If we don't resolve this conflict, what will be the outcome, and what will it mean for you?*

Learn from the Past and Build Organizational Alignment

> *5 - What insights have you learned during this conversation?*

> *6 - What will you promise to do, by when, to be in alignment to achieve our shared vision?*

Seek Accountability to Champion Execution Habits

> 7 - What are the "if, then" habits you will put into practice to keep the promises we just made?

> 8 - How and when will you seek accountability to verify you are in alignment?

STEP 4

Seek Accountability to Champion Execution Habits

Seek Mutual Trust, Respect and Accountability

Execute New Habits for Accelerating Growth Momentum

Seek Mutual Trust, Respect and Accountability

Are you one of those people who can overcome distractions and routinely remain focused so that you accomplish what is most important?

Congratulations! Very few of us could answer "Yes" to that question. It's a given. Most of us are crazy busy, and even if your organization has wonderful visionary goals, many of your colleagues are probably juggling many other, less important goals all at once.

That means you can help your teammates, who miss opportunities routinely, to seize the right moments to act on the most important goals, because they are simply failing to notice these missed opportunities.

This chapter references Heidi Grant Halvorson's article in the *Harvard Business Review*, "Get Your Team to Do What It Says It's Going to Do: How to close the gap between knowing and doing."[77] The focus is on what it takes to create and act on new, more effective execution habits that are designed to seize the moments of opportunity to do what matters most and achieve results, routinely and consistently.

Why is this so important? Because it's so easy to be swamped by the ocean of distractions from previous habits.

You have formed habits when dealing with coworkers, emails, phone calls, meetings and project management, to name a few. Hopefully, you have a lot of highly productive habits.

However, we all have habits that are unproductive. You know what I mean. Really.

As Heidi questions in her article:

> Have you ever not had time to follow up on an important priority? Was there no chance at all to put extra effort in finishing a challenging report?

> Did you ever procrastinate and put off doing something important, just because it was inconvenient and uncomfortable?

> Really, you didn't have time to work out?[78]

Hopefully, you get the point.

Act on New Habits to Do What Matters Most to Achieve the Shared Vision

Here's the deal. What if you could develop new habits to make it easier to stay focused with laser-like precision? What if you could focus on critical actions to achieve the most important priorities and to make the best and most effective use of your time?

Let's explore this by asking another question:

> Why have you been so successful in reaching some of your goals but not others? If you aren't sure why, you're far from alone in your confusion.

It turns out that even very brilliant, highly accomplished people are pretty lousy when it comes to understanding why they succeed or fail.[79]

This question and comment come from Heidi Grant Halvorson in her book *9 Things Successful People Do Differently.*

Just wanting to be more productive and champion execution isn't enough to make you, or any of your colleagues, more productive.

You need to find a way to deal effectively with previous habits you have developed, especially when swamped with distractions, interruptions and having just way too much on your plate.

Fortunately, there is a very simple strategy that has been proven to work by using what motivational scientists at the NeuroLeadership Institute call "if-then" planning.[80]

"If-then" planning is a scientifically validated, simple and powerful tool to develop new execution habits.

When you Champion Execution Habits, you create and sustain new productive habits and routines to seize moments to do what matters most.

Heidi Halvorson's article also states that well over one hundred studies—measuring such things as turning in weekly reports promptly; exercising regularly; taking medication on schedule; managing time effectively—have shown that deciding, in advance, when and where you will take specific actions to reach your goals can double or triple your chances for success.

Here is a simple example:

> If it is 2 p.m. on Friday, then I will email Charlie an update and progress report.

Now the cue for "2 p.m. on Friday" is directly wired into your brain to the action "email Charlie."

"If-then" planning is a technique of mindfulness, just below your conscious awareness. Through "if-then" planning, you will begin to mindfully scan the environment for it. As a result, you will seize the critical moment—at 2 p.m. on Friday—to send the report, even though you are busy doing other things.

Once you are aware of the "if" part of the plan, the mind triggers the "then" part.

You will begin to execute the plan without having to think much about it, even when occupied with other projects. Otherwise, when you are entrenched in existing habits, paralyzed by cognitive overload from too many tasks to remember, or simply too distracted, you will tend to forget to execute what is most important.

Peter Gollwitzer, the psychologist who first studied "if-then" planning, has described it as creating "instant habits." Unlike many of our other habits, these don't get in the way of our goals; rather, they help us achieve them.[81]

Making "if-then" plans to tackle your current projects is probably the single most effective thing you can do to ensure success and champion execution.

The Formula: If "X" Happens, Then I Will Do "Y"

Let's check in on your instincts about the impact of this practice to keep your commitments.

More than 50 percent of the time, we fail to follow through on the commitments mentioned. Even when we know what we need to do, and we truly want and intend to do it, somehow it still doesn't happen. Why? We allow competing goals, motivations and temptations to interfere.

Here are three more examples of the "if-then" formula from Dr. Halvorson:

1. **If I haven't written the report before lunch, then I will make it the first thing I do when I return.**

2. **If I am getting too distracted by colleagues, then I will stick to a five-minute chat limit and head back to work.**

3. **If it is 6 p.m., then I will spend an hour working out in the company gym before heading home.**[82]

How effective are these plans?

By using "if-then" planning to tackle your goals, you will also want to discuss the real challenges and obstacles that might derail you.

Studies from the NeuroLeadership Institute show

that people who decide, in advance, how they will deal with such snags—i.e., avoid frazzle—are much more resilient and able to stay on track to build new execution habits.[83]

Those who skip planning for the inevitable bumps in the road and unforeseen complications are more prone to become frazzled.

Commit to Meeting Rhythms for Accountability and Feedforward

Many of the goals you struggle with, at work and in your personal life, have one thing in common: the need for self-awareness, self-management and the willpower to resist temptations.

When faced with a boring expense report or a dense white paper, it takes self-control to avoid checking Facebook, answering email, or firing up a game of solitaire.

And, as we learned from the Productive Conflict Profile, no matter what your style, it takes even more strength of will to keep negative, judgmental and biased automatic thoughts in check.

Let's check in to remember what we learned from the Productive Conflict Profile. Which of these two statements best describes you?

1. If I have automatic thoughts that lead to destructive conflict, then I change my thoughts and practice productive conflict solutions.

Congratulations! You have developed an effective new habit to address differences of opinion with others you work with by practicing productive conflict. Keep up the good work.

2. It is challenging to practice productive conflict solutions.

If you think this way, it is suggested you become more self-aware of your automatic thoughts. Say to yourself, "If I recognize automatic thoughts, then I will step back, change my thoughts and practice productive conflict."

Your capacity for self-awareness to recognize automatic thoughts, step back and change your thoughts is not unlike the muscles in your body.

Like biceps or triceps, the willpower to be self-managing can vary in strength, not only from person to person but from moment to moment. Just as well-developed biceps sometimes get tired and jelly-like after a strenuous workout, so does your willpower muscle. The good news is that willpower depletion is only temporary. In-The-Moment Conversations has a built-in mechanism to lift the spirits, especially when the pressure is on and rest is not an option.

Execute New Habits for Accelerating Growth Momentum

- When you Regain Focus, you become mindful and restore the willpower you and your team must have to face the real challenges before you.

- When you Craft a Shared Vision, you will be re-energized to reach your Mount Everest and fulfill a higher purpose.

- When you Build Organizational Alignment, make sure everyone is rowing in the same direction.

- When you Champion Execution Habits, "if-then" planning makes it much more likely that you and your team will achieve its goals by providing a bridge between intentions and reality!

Motivational scientists continue to do the research, and the data shows that "if-then" goal planning fosters ownership and essentially reprograms people to execute consistently.

Be committed to practice In-The-Moment Conversations. Transform moments of lack of willpower into moments of inspiration to face your real challenges!

Case Study for STEP 4

"Scott," I said, "now let's complete **STEP 4**. I am curious to know what has been most important for you since you have experienced this In-The-Moment Conversation?"

"I have discovered how important it is to clear my head," Scott replied, "listen more deeply, and bring out the best in myself and others."

After summarizing, I shared, "I have discovered that

you are open for change. Jim Collins once said, the x factor for leaders is humility.[84] You demonstrated that."

I asked Scott, "What are the new 'if-then' habits you will put into practice to keep the promises we just made? Furthermore, how and when will you seek accountability to verify you are in alignment?"

Scott said, "OK, let me try this out. If I recognize an uncomfortable feeling from my automatic thoughts about another person, then I will speak up and say, 'Do you have a moment? I have something on my mind that I need your help with.'

"I will seek accountability with you and with my team. I will let them know that I am accountable to practice this new habit."

Well done! This stuff does work.

Eight Accelerator Questions Guide

- Establish an agreement to meet at a certain time and place to give a few moments of undivided attention for increased awareness and insights.

- Practice "Listen to Learn; Ask to Empower" to make it safe for your colleague to speak up. Remember to summarize often by reflecting on what is being said.

- Each of you will ask these questions out loud for your colleague to answer candidly.

Seize the Moment and Regain Focus

1 - What's on your mind, that needs to be addressed, or put aside, to be fully present and focused?

2 - What is the conflict, and what is the real challenge for you?

Remember the Future and Craft a Shared Vision

3 - What is the ideal outcome, and what will it mean for you to achieve it?

4 - If we don't resolve this conflict, what will be the outcome, and what will it mean for you?

Learn from the Past and Build Organizational Alignment

5 - What insights have you learned during this conversation?

6 - What will you promise to do, by when, to be in alignment to achieve our shared vision?

Seek Accountability to Champion Execution Habits

7 - What are the "if, then" habits you will put into practice to keep the promises we just made?

8 - How and when will you seek accountability to verify you are in alignment?

Part 5

Go Deeper

Why the Cultures That Work Team?

We have done the research. We have scaled up cultures. We lead global businesses. We have been in the trenches with thousands of employees. We have professional certifications and degrees. We are the best in the world at what is unique for us: Mindful Leadership at Every Level – In-The-Moment Conversations productive conflict solutions.

We exceed a total of 60,000 hours as executive coaches, trainers and educators for over 250 midmarket firms.

We are business owners. We have trained hundreds of business owners, family businesses, corporate presidents, CEOs, COOs, CFOs and CMOs. We have influenced thousands of employees. We are passionate about equipping you with the tools you need to accelerate thru conflict!

Our Cultures That Work Team makes it easier to have the harder conversations, before it's too late;

before employees disengage, performance slips and your business growth will lose momentum.

In-The-Moment Conversations makes all the difference for executive teams, managers, and leaders throughout organizations who are facing the natural friction, confusion, and underperformance when scaling up.

These conversations are essential. Put them into practice before it's too late, before leaders must revert to crisis conversations.

When colleagues at every level of the organization are in strategic alignment, they will seek accountability to do what matters most. Employee engagement will soar, and your company culture will accelerate the momentum of business growth.

Log on to Culturesthatwork.com/accelerate-thru-conflict/

Learn how you and your colleagues can to go deeper by…

1. Taking advantage of complimentary support and resources

2. Ordering bulk discounted books for your culture

3. Gaining access to the Productive Conflict Profile

4. Discovering the benefits of Mindful Leadership at Every Level training

5. Learning about becoming a certified facilitator

Inspiration for Training Using These Tools

USI Insurance Services (USI) is approaching $2 billion in revenue with more than 7,000 associates in approximately 200 offices across the country.

Scott Chisholm is the Property and Casualty Practice Leader for USI, at their Carmel, Indiana, office.

Scott sent a remarkably clear email to his team that was engaged with our course Mindful Leadership at Every Level, In-The-Moment Conversations live and virtual training.

Scott gave us permission to share with you his insightful email to the Property and Casualty Team located in 4 offices in Indiana:

Property and Casualty Team:

Thank you for dedicating the time on Monday & Tuesday to take a step back and evaluate a closer introspective look at your own style, motivators, and triggers. For some, the DISC results were a surprise to see their true characteristics out in the open. For others, it was affirmation of the things they already knew about themselves—and have identified as a growth opportunity. Either way, the pursuit of a mastery of self-awareness is critical in the workplace. Below are my observations from the workshops.

1. Knowing yourself makes life a lot easier. *When interviewing candidates, one of the questions I am most interested in is "Tell me more about yourself." It's fascinating, the variety of answers you receive— everything from direct, results-driven feedback from the "D" to longer, drawn out stories about family, hardships, and work experience from the "S". Regardless, if you understand yourself, your requirements, and your defaults/automatic thoughts, it makes the resolution and overcoming conflict much easier. This workshop isn't meant to recreate or shift your style, but to accept and maximize it.*

2. Conflict can be a healthy strategic discipline. *When there is a lack of trust within a team, people are afraid to be vulnerable and share how they feel for fear of exposing their weaknesses. The USI culture promotes a collaborative approach to achieve collective goals. Contributions from the group are welcomed and encouraged.* **Psychological safety** *is celebrated and expected. Without the input, there is little enthusiasm, passion or excitement present. When this happens, there is no growth. People get complacent and we don't achieve our goals—status quo is accepted. By harnessing the positive energy in conflict, the relationship is strengthened.*

3. *Building new muscle memory takes practice.* When you drive a car, ride a bike, type on the computer—you don't think consciously about how you are going to do it. You just do it. You just perform these tasks because you have developed muscle memory. Equipped with the self-awareness of your own style, triggers, and defaults with conflict + an awareness about those you work with ... it takes practice to make the most out of your daily interactions. Those who truly have a desire to improve the relationships in their life will take pride in this journey. Work should be fun. It starts with an acceptance of being the best version of yourself. This is why I'm excited to work in mini-teams—to practice. To quote Vince Lombardi, "It is harder to break a good habit then it is a bad one."

Acknowledgments

Mike and Craig, co-founders of Cultures That Work, Inc., are deeply grateful for our team: Monica Roberts, Dan Hurley, and Pamela Carrington-Rotto, PhD.

The CTW team could not possibly write this book nor deliver on our live and 24/7 virtual training without our team partnership with Dunbar Organizational Health: David Dann; Nick Dann; Chuck Duke; Thad Perry, PhD; and Jennifer Tabor and her team.

We are grateful for the business owners and their executive leadership teams who were the real life laboratory where we discovered this knowledge: The Montrow Group; Brent Tilson and the Tilson Team; Jeff Kittle and the HKP Senior Management and Key Leadership Team; Tag Birge and Andrew Held and the Birge & Held Leadership Team; Tag Birge and the Cornerstone Management team; David Eskenazi and the Sandor Development Team; Todd and Spencer Atkins and The Atkins Group Team; Drs. Michael and Michelle Edwards and the American Dental

Network Team; Dr. John Ladd and the Ladd Dental Team; Dr. Mok, Dr. Atanasovski, Theresa LaBranche, Traci Grossman and the Allure Medical Team; Doug Bowen and the Bowen Engineering Team; Mark Riggle and Charlie Meyer and the Threefold Partners; JJ Darr and the Certa Pro Indy Team; Joel Bell and the Whitehat Team; Lin Behnken and the Certa Pro Dayton Team; Marcus Hall and the California Closets Team; Matt Rolfsen and the Renovia Team; John Spegele and the GSS Team; Mark and Melissa Wahl and the Cobblestone Homes Team; Bill Dahm and the Crew Carwash Team; Bryan Barrett and the Barrett & Stokely Owners and Leadership Team; Scott Chisholm and the USI Property and Casualty Team; Santiago Jaramillo and the Emplify Team; Keith Cupp and the Gravitas Impact Coaches; Shannon Susko and the Metronome Team; Ari Weinzweig and the ZingTrain Team; Andy Bailey and the Aligntoday Team; Verne Harnish and the Scaling Up Certified Coaches; and Daniel Marcos and the Growth Institute Team.

About the Authors

Dr. Craig Overmyer

Dr. Craig Overmyer is an Executive Leadership Coach, ScalingUp Certified Coach, Cultural Transformation Tools Consultant, Results Certified Coach through the NeuroLeadership Institute, Keynote Speaker, and member of the National Speakers Association.

From 1985–1999, Craig Overmyer, D. Min, served as a pastoral counselor at St. Vincent Stress Center. In 1999, Craig became a trainer for RealTime Coaching.

From 2006 until 2011, Craig was a Senior Consultant for Chorus, Inc. and worked with the team led by Mike Evans. Craig is a Master Coach for the Hallmarks of Excellence in Leadership.

Craig is an author who has contributed to 6 books: *Success Is a Decision of the Mind; Dynamic Health; Getting Well; Never Too Old to Rock n' Roll-Life: After 50 The Best Years Yet;* and contributed ideas for the best seller *ScalingUp: How a Few Companies*

Make It...and Why the Rest Don't by Verne Harnish and the team at Gazelles.

Craig lives in Zionsville, Indiana, with his wife Becky who owns The Silk Purse Antiques, and volunteers at St. Luke's United Methodist Church.

Mike Montgomery

Mike Montgomery is founder and owner of Montrow Tool and Machine, Inc., CMD Mfg. Inc. and Industrial Interests, Inc. Mike also conducts business with partners in China, Vietnam and Japan.

Mike scaled up his company and achieved Growth 100 status in 1999. Mike and his team have developed a global firm through a culture that values candid conversations through leadership at every level.

Mike is free from being sucked into the drama of daily operations, and the shop runs without his interventions in the midst of "friction, confusion and underperformance."

About the Cultures That Work Team

We have delivered training to thousands of owners, C-suite executive leaders, executive leadership teams, department heads, managers, supervisors, team leaders and frontline staff for businesses of all sizes including multinational firms. Here are the team members:

Pamela Carrington-Rotto has earned a PhD in Clinical Psychology. Pamela is also a Scaling Up Certified Coach. She has a history as a CEO and a COO.

Pamela has scaled up not-for-profits as well as midmarket growth firms with hundreds of employees in her role as CEO and COO.

Pamela and I have formed a special niche in the commercial real estate industry. She is a colleague and mentor who has done the hard work to learn how to make In-The-Moment Conversations easier for everyone.

Dan Hurley, a Scaling Up Certified Coach, comes with an extensive business background that includes 30 years as an executive in automobile manufacturing industries. Dan has led hundreds of executive leaders and has served as a Vistage Chair.

Dan and I have teamed up in offering public workshops and trained the Mindful Leadership at Every Level In-The-Moments Conversations in Michigan.

Monica Roberts is our Director of Operations who has extensive history in the aerospace and manufacturing industries and cultural transformation tools.

About Our Partners

Dunbar Organizational Health Partnership

We established a Strategic Alliance Agreement with Bill Dunbar and Associates, LLC which operates the Division called Dunbar Organizational Health (Dunbar Org. Health). David Dann, CEO, and Nick Dann, Managing Director, invested in and supported our work through a virtual training platform that affords the opportunity to have a global reach.

Chuck Duke is the Producer of all of our video content that you can access through links in this book. Dr. Thad Perry, Adjunct Professor at the University of Tennessee, is an expert in researching and understanding the impact of employee engagement, disengagement and turnover.

The Dunbar Org. Health team delivers our facilitator certification training and live events.

We also have developed a virtual platform that is accessible 24/7 for highly interactive and engaging education and training that makes learning stick!

The Dunbar Org. Health team will be hosting the free virtual demonstration videos and podcasts offered to anyone who buys this book.

Emplify Employee Engagement Partnership

In 2017 we became a strategic partner with Emplify, the world leader in assessing and developing employee engagement.

Santiago Jaramillo, cofounder of Emplify, is the author of the book *Agile Engagement.*

Santiago, Adam, Nicole, Nikki and others are the amazing team that provides me with the extraordinary ability to really measure employee engagement for companies that I serve and provide direction and coaching to transform disengaged employees into engaged, highly productive employees.

Endnotes

INTRODUCTION

1. Jim Collins, "How Does Your Flywheel Turn? A Good to Great® Strategic Tool," *Jim Collins* (website), 2017, https://www.jimcollins.com/tools/How-does-your-flywheel-turn.pdf.

2. Brené Brown, *Dare to Lead: Brave Work. Tough Conversations. Whole Hearts* (New York: Random House, 2018).

3. Denise Lee Yohn, *Fusion: How Integrating Brand and Culture Powers the World's Greatest Companies* (Boston: Nicholas Brealey, 2018).

4. Patrick Lencioni, *The Five Dysfunctions of a Team: A Leadership Fable* (San Francisco: Jossey-Bass, 2002).

5. David Rock, Beth Jones, and Chris Weller, "Using Neuroscience to Make Feedback Work and Feel Better," *Strategy+Business,* (website), August 27, 2018, https://www.strategy-business.com/article/Using-Neuroscience-to-Make-Feedback-Work-and-Feel-Better.

6. Verne Harnish, *Mastering the Rockefeller Habits: What You Must Do to Increase the Value of Your Growing Firm* (Ashburn: Gazelles Inc., 2002).

7. Rock, Jones, and Weller, "Using Neuroscience."

8. Richard Boyatzis, Melvin Smith, and Ellen Van Oosten, *Helping People Change: Coaching with Compassion for Lifelong Learning and Growth* (Boston: Harvard Business Review Press, 2019).

9. Boyatzis, Smith, and Van Oosten, *Helping People Change*.

10. Rock, Jones, and Weller, "Using Neuroscience."

11. Verne Harnish, *Scaling Up: How a Few Companies Make It…and Why the Rest Don't* (Ashburn: Gazelles Inc., 2014).

12. Harnish, *Scaling Up*

PART 1: CONFLICT IMPACTS MOMENTUM

13. Craig E. Runde and Tim A. Flanagan, *Becoming a Conflict Competent Leader* (San Francisco: Jossey-Bass, 2012).

14. Collins, *"How Does Your Flywheel Turn?"*

15. Harnish, *Scaling Up*

16. Collins, *"How Does Your Flywheel Turn?"*

17. Jim Collins and Jerry I. Porras, *Built to Last: Successful Habits of Visionary Companies* (New York: HarperBusiness, 1994).

18. Harnish, *Mastering the Rockefeller Habits.*

19. Harnish, *Scaling Up*

20. Daniel Goleman, Richard Boyatzis, and Annie McKee, *Primal Leadership: Unleashing the Power of Emotional Intelligence* (Boston: Harvard Business Review Press, 2013).

21. Harnish, *Scaling Up*

22. Jim Collins, *Good to Great: Why Some Companies Make the Leap...and Others Don't* (New York: HarperBusiness, 2001).

23. John Wiley & Sons, Inc., "Everything DiSC® Productive Conflict Profile," discprofile (website), https://www.discprofile.com/products/everything-disc-productive-conflict/.

24. John Wiley & Sons, Inc., "Everything DiSC® Productive Conflict Profile."

25. John Wiley & Sons, Inc., "Everything DiSC® Productive Conflict Profile."

26. Harnish, *Scaling Up*

PART 2: TRANSFORM FRICTION INTO PRODUCTIVE CONFLICT

27. Alden Mills said this in a keynote address at the October 15, 2019 Scaling Up Summit in Anaheim, California.

28. Barrett Values Centre, "Improving Your Business through Values," *Barrett Values Centre* (website), August 2008, available at http://www.values-in-business.com/wp-content/uploads/2011/11/improving-your-business-thro-values-flier2.pdf.

29. John P. Kotter and James L. Heskett, *Corporate Culture and Performance* (New York: Free Press, 2011).

30. Collins and Porras, *Built to Last.*

31. Cultures That Work, example of *Cultural Values Assessment Report.*

32. Cultures That Work, *Cultural Values Assessment Report.*

33. Amy Gallo, *HBR Guide to Dealing with Conflict* (Boston: Harvard Business Review Press, 2017).

34. Daniel Coyle, *The Culture Code: The Secrets of Highly Successful Groups* (New York: Bantam, 2018).

35. Daniel Goleman, "The Hidden Opportunity in Conflicts at Work," *Korn Ferry Institute* (website), last updated March 12, 2018, https://www.kornferry.com/institute/conflict-management-opportunity-emotional-intelligence.

36. Howard M. Shore, *Your Business is a Leaky Bucket: Learn How to Avoid Losing Millions in Revenue and Profit Annually* (New York: Morgan James Publishing, 2017).

37. Shore, *Your Business is a Leaky Bucket.*

38. Brown, *Dare to Lead.*

39. Daniel Goleman, *The Brain and Emotional Intelligence: New Insights* (Florence, MA: More Than Sound, 2011).

PART 3: PREPARING FOR THE CONVERSATION

40. Chip Heath and Dan Heath, *The Power of Moments* (New York: Simon & Schuster, 2017).

41. Zak Keefer, "From 1–5 to playoffs' doorstep: Inside the players-only meeting that swung the Colts' 2018 season," *Indianapolis Star*, December 26, 2018.

42. Keefer, "From 1–5 to playoffs' doorstep."

43. Keefer, "From 1–5 to playoffs' doorstep."

44. Brown, *Dare to Lead.*

45. John Wiley & Sons, Inc., "Everything DiSC® Productive Conflict Profile." See https://www. discprofile .com/products/everything-disc-productive-conflict/ for an example of a Productive Conflict Profile Report.

46. Steven R. Covey, *The 7 Habits of Highly Effective People: Powerful Lessons in Personal Change* (New York: Free Press, 1989).

47. Ron Ernst, *RealTime Coaching* (Carmel, IN: Leadership Horizons, 1999).

48. Seth Godin, "90% of coaching is self-coaching," *Seth's Blog*, November 28, 2018, https://seths. blog/2018/11/90-of-coaching-is -self-coaching/.

49. Seth Godin, "90% of coaching."

50. Covey, *The 7 Habits.*

51. Michael Bungay Stanier, *The Coaching Habit: Say Less, Ask More & Change the Way You Lead Forever* (Toronto: Box of Crayons Press, 2016).

52. Brett Stetka, "How to Coach Like an Olympian: Winners embrace a psychologically nuanced approach to motivating athletes," *Scientific American Mind*, July/August 2016.

PART 4: MASTERING PRODUCTIVE CONFLICT SOLUTIONS

53. Ronald R. Reagan, "Address at Commencement Exercises at Eureka College, Eureka, Illinois," May 9, 1982, available at https://www.reaganfoundation. org/ronald-reagan/reagan-quotes-speeches/ commencement-address-eureka-college-1/.

STEP 1: SEIZE THE MOMENT AND REGAIN FOCUS

54. Daniel Goleman, *Focus: The Hidden Driver of Excellence,* (New York: Harper Paperbacks, 2015). First published 2013 by HarperCollins Publishers (New York).

55. Goleman, *Focus.*

56. NeuroLeadership Institute, "Brain-Based Coaching Engagements," Coach Folder.

57. Ari Weinzweig, "Secret #33 - Mindfulness Matters," excerpted pamphlet from The Guide to Good Leading Series, available at https://www. zingermanspress.com/our-books/the-secret-pamphlets.

58. See www.hallmarksofexcellence.com.

STEP 2: REMEMBER THE FUTURE AND CRAFT A SHARED VISION

59. James M. Kouzes and Barry Posner, "To Lead, Create a Shared Vision," *Harvard Business Review*, January 2009.

60. Kouzes and Posner, "To Lead, Create a Shared Vision."

61. David Anspaugh, dir. *Hoosiers*. Saginaw, MI: DeHaven Productions, 1986.

62. Richard E. Boyatzis, "When Pulling to the Negative Emotional Attractor Is Too Much or Not Enough to Inspire and Sustain Outstanding Leadership," in The Fulfilling Workplace, ed. Ronald J. Burke and Cary L. Cooper (Routledge, 2016).

63. Richard E. Boyatzis, "When Pulling to the Negative Emotional Attractor."

64. Paul Warner, "DecisionWise Benchmark Study Finds that 34% of Employees in the U.S. Do Not Speak Up Because of Fear of Retribution," *decisionwise* (website), last updated at February 8, 2012, https://decision-wise.com/decisionwise-benchmark-study/.

STEP 3: LEARN FROM THE PAST TO BUILD ORGANIZATIONAL ALIGNMENT

65. Lencioni, *The Five Dysfunctions of a Team.*

66.David P. Norton and Robert S. Kaplan, *The Balanced Scorecard: Translating Strategy into Action* (Boston: Harvard Business Review Press, 1996).

67. Goleman, *Focus.*

68. Amy F. T, Arnsten, "The Biology of Being Frazzled," *Science 280*, no. 5370, June 12, 1998,1711–1712.

69. Mark said this in a keynote address at the October 16, 2019 Scaling Up Summit in Anaheim, California.

70. Coyle, *The Culture Code.*

71. Coyle, *The Culture Code.*

72. David Scott Yeager et al., "Breaking the Cycle of Mistrust: Wise Interventions to Provide Critical Feedback Across the Racial Divide," *Journal of Experimental Psychology: General* 143, no. 2, 2014, 804–824.

73. Jack Welch, "Three Ways to Take Your Company's Pulse," *Jack Welch Winning* (website), May 5, 2015, www.jackwelch.strayer.edu/winning /three-ways-take-company-pulse (originally published on LinkedIn).

74. Santiago Jaramillo and Todd Richardson, *Agile Engagement: How to Drive Lasting Results by Cultivating a Flexible, Responsive, and Collaborative Culture* (Hoboken: Wiley, 2016).

75. Jason Barnaby, *Igniting the Fire Starter Within: The Secrets to Finding Your Fire, Fanning Your Flame & Tending Your Tribe* (CreateSpace Independent Publishing Platform, 2019).

76. Gary Chapman, *Everybody Wins: The Chapman Guide to Solving Conflicts without Arguing* (Carol Stream: Tyndale House Publishers Inc., 2007).

STEP 4: SEEK ACCOUNTABILITY TO CHAMPION EXECUTION HABITS

77. Heidi Grant Halvorson, "Get Your Team to Do What It Says It's Going to Do," *Harvard Business Review*, May 2014.

78. Halvorson, "Get Your Team."

79. Heidi Grant Halvorson, *9 Things Successful People Do Differently* (Boston: Harvard Business Review Press, 2012).

80. Halvorson, "Get Your Team."

81. Halvorson, "Get Your Team."

82. Halvorson, "Get Your Team."

83. David Rock, "Managing with the Brain in Mind," *Strategy+Business*, (website), August 27, 2009, https://www.strategy-business.com/article /09306 (originally published by Booz & Company).

84. Jim Collins, *Good to Great: Why Some Companies Make the Leap…and Others Don't* (New York: HarperBusiness, 2001).